MW00937371

The Orphan's Father

Dan Osterweil

Producer & International Distributor
eBookPro Publishing
www.ebook-pro.com

The Orphan's Father
Dan Osterweil

Copyright © 2022 Dan Osterweil

All rights reserved; No parts of this book may be reproduced or transmitted in any form or by any means, electronic or mechanical, including photocopying, recording, taping, or by any information retrieval system, without the author's explicit permission in writing.

Contact: tamar@zakut.com
ISBN 9798833231098

"This book is dedicated to the memory our parents, Dr Moshe (Monek) and Hella Osterweil, my unsung heroes; who taught us how to overcome adversity and reach out to help others"

THE ORPHAN'S FATHER

A Jewish Doctor's Inspiring WW2 Historical Novel,
Based on the True Story of a Holocaust Survivor

Dan Osterweil

CONTENTS

Preface

The events reported here — my family's experiences in one of the darkest periods of human history —are accounts as reported from living memory. Some conversations are reconstructed, and some of the wider context is based on my own research, but all personal experiences described here were reported to me by family members and friends who lived through them.

I began writing this story between Holocaust Remembrance Day and Israeli Memorial Day, which commemorates those who lost their lives to terrorism and in Israel's wars, beginning with the war for Israel's independence.

The timing made me reflect on how best to preserve our family's memories of the events I relate here, which happened more than seventy years ago, and to better understand the effect they had on me and on others born after the war. My parents and the other people described here have shaped me and continue to affect the way I look at this world, and I want those same influences to be available to the generations after me.

I probably should have done this twenty years ago, when more of the people involved in the events were still alive and available to corroborate the stories. I had my own life to lead, of course, and the topic was a difficult one. The circumstances, events, and people mentioned in this book put the spotlight on a very dark period in the history of Europe. For a long time, I could not get myself to do it.

One day in 1986 or 1987, out of the blue, I received a phone call from my cousin David Ladner, who lived at the time in Connecticut. David asked if I had seen the recent *The Holocaust: A History of the Jews of Europe During the Second World War*, by Sir Martin Gilbert;[1] after our phone call, he mailed me a copy. Gilbert's book mentioned Ottó Komoly, a Jew who had served in the Austro-Hungarian Army during the First World War and had been decorated for heroism. During the Second World War, the Hungarian authorities allowed Komoly to rent a number of buildings in the capital for the protection of Jewish children, under the aegis of the International Red Cross. He was helped (Gilbert noted) by two Polish Jews, Sholem Offenbach and a Dr. Osterweil, both of whom were refugees in Hungary at the time. Ultimately Komoly and his associates rented more than thirty-five buildings, in which they sheltered five thousand Jewish children. David Ladner was the first person who directed my attention to the importance of what my father, the Dr. Osterweil in question, had done during the war.

My father himself rarely spoke about the war. My mother did tell stories from those days, at times, but only after my father's premature death at age 67. Every visit, every long drive or trip abroad, became an opportunity for stories, which I recorded. Sometimes she repeated stories she had told me before. The chronology sometimes shifted, but the details never varied. As time went on her sense of urgency in passing on her memories grew, perhaps because her memory started to fail her, or because she feared she would not be around forever. I remember one storytelling instance from 1987. I

---

1   Published 1985.

had been invited to attend a medical conference in the United Kingdom, and I asked my mother to join me. A continental breakfast had just been wheeled into our Marriott Hotel room in London: rolls and croissants, butter and jam, tea. Out of nowhere, as she buttered a croissant, my mother started telling me of a time leading up to one of the deportations in the Jewish ghetto in Tarnów, Poland, an event she remembered and described in the minutest detail.

After a while, I noticed we were getting close to the time for a London sightseeing tour I had arranged. I suggested we get ready to go down to the lobby of the hotel. My mother stared at me intently. "Wait," she said. "I'm almost done with this chapter. The tour can wait."

My research continued, over the course of our normal busy lives, for over twenty-five years. Digging into my family's personal experience during one of the most atrocious acts in human history is not something one does lightly or easily. When I shared some of the stories with family and friends, they insisted that they should be told to a wider audience. I had frequent conversations with my sister, Ewa, who also encouraged me to write up the results of my investigations. My older daughter, Gali, mailed me a book by Izhak Kashti, a professor of education at Tel Aviv University and an authority on the history of education among Hungarian Jews.[2] It described the rescue of children in Hungary, with details mentioning my father and the safe houses that he, with the help of others, established. My family's wartime history started coalescing in my mind.

I became convinced that producing this document was something I should do, for three reasons. First, I owe this to my family, most especially to my parents. My mother never said so explicitly,

2   The title of the book, published in Hebrew, translates as *Rescue as Protest and Rebellion: Jewish Children's Houses in Hungary, 1944–1945* (Resling, 2014).

but she clearly felt an increasingly urgent need to have our family history recorded. The things she told me over the years amount to an oral history and make her a co-author of this work. I felt an obligation, too, to my immediate family: my wife, children, grandchildren, sister, brother, nieces, nephews, cousins, and all of our descendants to come.

Second, while popular remembrance of the Holocaust tends to focus on evil villains and selfless heroes, those circumstances, events, and people were all more complex than they are generally portrayed as being. The overall experience of that time for most people was one of absolute chaos. It was nearly impossible to know, at any given moment, who was good and who was evil, what choice would mean survival and what choice would mean death. Much of the time success in those fateful choices depended largely on luck. That terrifying environment brought out the worst in some people, and the best in others. Some people did manage to show their humanity, even in the midst of evil and chaos. It seems to have brought out much of the best in my parents, and in the many, many people who helped them along the way, some of whom did not survive. I have written this book partly to let people know about their heroism, because I am proud, not just of my family, but also of the great things human beings are capable of in terrible circumstances. Yet my father, in one of the rare occasions he spoke of it, told me that most survivors had details they wanted to hide about the circumstances of how they survived and what "collateral damage" their efforts may have done to others.

Finally, this book is meant to serve as a warning. The rise of nationalism in Poland and Hungary is eerily evocative of the 1930s. Similar currents are noticeable now even in the United States. History is filled with the persecution and murder of those who are guilty only of being different: in appearance, in gender preferences, in religious faith, in language or customs. Refugees are once again much in the news. This reminds me that my family and people, too, were refugees, and makes me acutely uncomfortable to see how these modern refugees are being treated. The big difference was that for us, there was a dream and then a hope of return to our own homeland, which would replace the countries we fled from. We owe it to our children and the children who follow them to tell them of humankind's worst deeds and of ways to prevent and resist them. This is a large part of the reason for writing about my parents, Monek and Hela, and their experiences during a war that showed how terrifyingly low human beings can sink when they do not stand up to repression and evil.

Prologue

When the time came for me to become a bar mitzvah, my family lived in Rishon Lezion, then a smallish town near Tel Aviv where everybody seemed to know everybody else. A synagogue on the hill overlooking the town was built in 1886. It was there I was to deliver my haftarah, my readings during the ceremony.

It was a Saturday morning in April, and our home on the west side of town was about a half hour walk to the synagogue. We got up early, but it was already hot. We had no air-conditioning to cool the heat of the day's *chamsin*, the dry wind coming from the desert. Anxious to be on time, I urged my father to hurry.

He gave me a pained, small grin. "It's okay. We have time. We're driving there."

I was shocked. Driving on Shabbat was forbidden by rabbinic law. We were going to ignore our beliefs and drive on a Saturday to the synagogue for my *bar mitzvah*?

"Look," he explained, seeing my stunned expression. "I'm too tired to walk. It's too hot and it's uphill. So, I'm driving. If you want, join us. If not, you can walk."

We drove.

After I delivered my *aliyah*, in the early evening, we had a celebration in our large backyard to honor my entering manhood. There were many people there and I was allowed to drink some cognac, which made me a little tipsy. It was a very enjoyable day.

The next day, I recall relaxing on my parents' bed alongside my father. I asked him, "Abba, what was that about yesterday, when you said you wanted to drive on the Sabbath, the day of my *bar mitzvah*? Isn't that wrong?"

He stood up and gave me a gentle smile. "Danny, you wanted to follow the ritual, do a *bar mitzvah*. I supported you. I knew you wanted your friends there. But did you ever ask me how I felt about it, whether I cared about it?"

I couldn't understand what he was getting at. "No," I answered.

"If you had asked me," my father confessed, "I would have told you that I don't care about or believe in all that. For me, there is no God."

This made no sense at all. I knew his grandmother had wanted him to be a rabbi, and that he had pursued the study of philosophy before he had gone to medical school. The idea that he was an atheist was incomprehensible.

"Why?"

He paused, searching for the right words. "To me, God was a great power of nature, a supernatural phenomenon, a kind of power that controls what we humans do, how we behave. The principle is that people who believe in God will follow an appropriate and human behavior. But during my imprisonment in the concentration camp during the war, I saw things that convinced me that God does not exist. If He did exist, those things would not have happened."

My father rarely told me any details about his wartime experiences, but he chose that moment to tell me about one incident that I relate below, in which he witnessed the execution of a group of Jewish children by the SS. Afterwards, he made a vow to himself. If he survived the camp and the war, he would dedicate a year of his life to helping and protecting children in need.

It wasn't until much later that I learned that he had done that and more, beginning long before the war was over and putting his own survival very much at risk.

PART ONE: POLAND

CHAPTER 1

Before the War

My father, Monek Osterweil, was born to a family of tailors in Tarnów, a small city in southeastern Poland, on May 26, 1903. He was one of five children of Israel Jakub Osterweil and Taube Zelnik. His three brothers were named Herman, Aron, and Ushier, and his sister was named Ruzia. Aron and Ushier followed in their father's footsteps as tailors, while Herman started his own business.

Monek and his siblings went to Polish public schools, where he obtained a broad education both in Polish and in German. Poland could be a problematic place for Jews, and when my father was young there was growing interest among people he knew to settle in the area then known as Palestine. Monek learned Hebrew in the youth movement called Hashomer Hatzair ("The Young Guard"), the first Zionist youth organization, founded in Europe in 1913 to embody a humanistic interpretation of Judaism and Zionism. The movement's leader, Meir Ya'ari, an educator, social activist, and later member of the Israeli Knesset, encouraged young people to learn agricultural techniques so that the Jewish homeland could sustain a new nation. Hashomer Hatzair now operates in twenty-one countries around the world. Monek became one of the leaders of the Tarnów chapter, which held meetings in my grandparents' home.

In the 1920s, the leaders of Hashomer Hatzair were encouraging all members to go to Palestine as soon as possible to be farmers, but my father was always independent in his thinking, and this was one area in which he disagreed with the leadership. Monek thought that some members should further their education first, in order to be helpful in other ways. His influence was significant enough that this idea became known within the movement as Osterweilism:[3] many delayed their *aliyah* (immigration) to Palestine to obtain degrees as agronomists or business experts first. This caused some friction with some of my father's colleagues, but he was never a person who was easily persuaded to change his mind.

Monek lived in Tarnów, as did his siblings. Ushier and Aron would become tailors. Herman would have first a metal-appraisal business and then a shirt factory called OPE. Monek was clearly more of an intellectual. In 1922, he moved to Kraków, where he studied philosophy at the university, largely in deference to his grandmother. She had wanted him to be a rabbi, but he did not feel drawn to the profession; studying philosophy was as much of a concession as he was willing to make. His father wanted Monek to be a physician, and medicine did appeal to him, so after he finished his studies in philosophy, he set out on that path. Because there were numerous restrictions imposed on Jewish applicants to Polish universities, he decided to pack up and go to Italy, where he had a better chance of accomplishing his goals. He graduated from the

---

3   The term *Osterweilism* was coined by economist David Horowitz, later governor of the Israel Central Bank. He was an early member of Hashomer Hatzair in Galicia and immigrated to Palestine in the nineteen thirties.

university in Perugia in medicine and surgery on July 14, 1931, with a perfect score in the final exam, 110 out of 110. His best grades were in biological studies and clinical topics. When he came back to Poland, he worked first as a doctor in the Jewish hospital in Tarnów, specializing in pediatrics, then got a better job at the Jewish hospital in Kraków, also in pediatrics.

One of Hashomer Hatzair's meetings my father attended in Tarnów took place at the home of Sala Ladner, a woman about my father's age who volunteered her parents' home for the purpose. It was at that meeting that he first noticed Sala's beautiful younger sister, Hela. She, too, had joined the movement, attracted by the ideals and inspired by her sister's involvement. This is how my parents, Monek Osterweil and Hela Ladner, first met.

Hela Ladner was born in 1909 in Borek, a small town not far from Tarnów. She was the youngest of seven siblings in a family of mostly secular Jews. She had three sisters, Rozia, Rena, Regina (Rena), and Sala, and three brothers, Herman, Fredek, and Oskar. Her parents were Leon Ladner and Cywia (Munderer) Ladner. Their income came from leasing apartments and stores and from trading lumber. When my mother was small, the family owned a small foundry in the town of Bochnia, where they produced Christian paraphernalia, such as crosses and small statues of saints. My grandmother Cywia was a housewife. They moved from Bochnia to Tarnów in 1918, where they lived in a comfortable apartment on Targowa Street.

Like my father, my mother attended elementary Polish public school and Hebrew high schools. In addition to Polish and German, she also studied English. She learned Hebrew in Hashomer Hatzair and in Hebrew school.

Hela's father objected to her joining Hashomer Hatzair, out of concern that it would negatively impact her studies. To apply pressure, he held back paying her high school tuition, but Hela insisted on joining anyway. She financed her high school costs by giving private lessons tutoring other students. She proudly refused her father's money when, impressed by her determination, he later offered to pay. She became very involved with the movement and was even assigned to lead one of the *hachsharot* (work camps) for youngsters who came from other parts of Poland to be trained for the challenges in Palestine. The work on the farms, however, was incredibly hard, and when the young people complained, they were rebuffed rather than being reassured. My mother recalled one leader of Hashomer Hatzair in Poland telling her, "If you think this is rough, wait until you get to Palestine. It's much worse there, with all the fleas and mosquitoes and swamps."

Hela went to Italy to attend university at the same time Monek did. While he was intensely focused on his medical studies in Perugia, she stayed in Florence. She was a lively and vivacious young woman who loved parties and attention, but she was also exceptionally smart, graduating from the University of Florence on June 12, 1929, with a degree in philosophy and a scholastic score of 95 out of 110 possible points.

Showing her usual courage and determination, my mother left Italy to visit friends in Palestine despite rioting by Arabs trying to halt the Jewish settlements there during the late 1920s. Her friends were involved in the burgeoning Zionist movement, as members of Hashomer Hatzair, and she insisted on helping them. My father, however, attempted to lure the love of his life back to Poland. He wrote to Hela, suggesting that her mother's health was failing and that her family could use Hela's help.

When my mother, good daughter that she was, returned to Europe, she learned that her parents were not doing so badly. She was angry at first, but Monek found a way to soothe her resentment, explaining how much he loved and missed her when she was in Palestine. Apparently, he convinced her. She returned to Poland and agreed to marry him. (I have no details or documents about their wedding. Any photographs were lost during the war.) Hela continued working after they were married, teaching at kindergartens in Tarnów (1930–1934) and in Kraków (1934–1939).

My sister, Ewa, was born in Kraków in May of 1938, the only child of happy, doting parents, a pediatrician and a kindergarten teacher. Kraków was a vibrant community, rich in culture and tradition, and Monek, Hela, and Ewa were surrounded by Hela's extended family. By the next year, however, almost every aspect of that secure, pleasant life my mother was born into would be threatened. In a few years, much of it would be destroyed.

CHAPTER 2

Surviving the Soviets in Lwów

The fate of Poland was determined by a non-aggression agreement, signed in secret between Hitler's Germany and Stalin's Soviet Union. On August 23, 1939, the foreign ministers of Germany and the Soviet Union signed the Molotov-Ribbentrop Pact, which divided up European countries into Germany and Soviet spheres of influence. On September 1, Germany invaded Poland from the north-and southwest. Less than three weeks later, on September 17, Stalin ordered the Soviet invasion of Poland from the east.

My parents and sister were living in Kraków when the invasion of Poland took place. Hela was teaching kindergarten. Monek was working in the pediatric clinic of the Jewish hospital. He had been drafted as a medical officer into the Kraków Army (Armia Krajowa), which had been assembled back in the spring, on March 29, 1939. On the day of the Polish invasion, the Kraków Army had 90 tanks and 44 planes, which were no match for the *panzer* division (tanks) and *Luftwaffe* (air force) of Germany. The Kraków Army joined forces with the Lodz Army, but they were not enough to halt the German assault pouring into Poland.

As Nazi forces attacking from the west overran the Polish Seventh Infantry Division and headed for the center of the country, Monek and his garrison moved east, toward the region the Russians had occupied, and found themselves in the area around Lwów (called Lemberg by the Germans). Lwów was a historic center of culture in Poland and a source of great pride to the people. Now in Ukraine and renamed Lviv, it is on the list of UNESCO historic cities. It served as the home for many who later became famous for their accomplishments in diverse fields: actor Paul Muni, philosopher Martin Buber, classical pianist Emanuel Ax, Yiddish author and playwright Sholem Aleichem, and Holocaust survivor and Nazi hunter Simon Wiesenthal.

When the Nazis invaded in early September, the city of Lwów put up a great and honorable fight, forcing the Germans to surround it and wait for reinforcements. The Poles used both local volunteers and refugees to hold off the enemy, demonstrating exceptional bravery during the siege. On September 17, the 6th Red Army of the Ukrainian Front crossed the border just east of Lwów. Two days later, the first armored units from the Soviets reached the outskirts of the city. Again, showing admirable resistance, the fighters in Lwów fought furiously, using barricades and fortifications built by local residents, supervised by military engineers.

But it was hopeless. The Soviets sent seven field armies, numbering between 500,000 and one million men, pouring across Poland's eastern border. Lwów was surrounded and had the military might of two nations threatening it. The rest of the country was already occupied. Russian envoys negotiated a surrender with the city of Lwów and made promises to allow soldiers who surrendered to them to leave the country, but the Soviets were no more reliable than the Nazis. They reneged on their agreement, and the secret police, the NKVD, began arresting all Polish officers in Lwów and sending them to gulags in the Soviet Union. Lwów had at least 45 synagogues and other Jewish houses of prayer in the city, some centuries old. The Golden Rose Synagogue, for example, had been built in 1582. Most of them were destroyed by the Nazis.

After the fall of Lwów, my father managed to avoid capture, moving about the outskirts of the city. It was not easy to stay undetected. While fleeing the fighting against the Germans in the west, Monek had seen the light-colored Soviet scout planes flying overhead, looking for Polish fighters. He managed to keep from being seen, but it was becoming more difficult. Traveling anywhere was dangerous, as the Red Army had military roaming not only Lwów but also the surrounding countryside, trying to capture any Polish military who had melded into the general population.

Monek managed to befriend a fellow Pole who lived in the area of Lwów. This man had seen and heard messages from the occupying Soviet troops, who drove around in jeeps announcing that Polish professionals, such as teachers and doctors, were invited to a meeting in the center of Lwów. Monek asked if he thought he should attend the meeting and offer his medical expertise. "It doesn't smell good," said his Polish friend, in the vernacular of the time, so my father stayed away.

The man also shared stories he had heard of Soviet soldiers who had shot civilians for no other reason than to take their watches. If you are stopped by a Red Army patrol and asked to put your arms in the air, the man advised Monek, hold your sleeves with closed fists to hide your watch. There was so much fear in Poland that it would have been hard to separate the horror stories from reality, and to know if it was true that a man could be murdered for nothing more than a wristwatch.

My father was fortunate to have met his Polish friend and protector. They learned later that many doctors and teachers had showed up at that meeting at the city hall in Lwów, volunteering to help the Red Army. They were promptly rounded up, taken away, and gunned down. Because the Polish system of military conscription required every university graduate who did not have an exemption to become a military reserve officer, there was a huge number of men the Soviets considered military rather than civilian. The Red Army also sought to apprehend people they considered to be the intelligentsia in Polish society. Anyone with a formal education, in the eyes of the Soviets, became an enemy of the occupation.

The Soviet offensive took control of a huge portion of Poland, more than 200,000 square kilometers of land, home to 13.5 million Poles. Though the Soviet Politburo called their invasion a "liberation campaign," it was done by agreement with Germany, as was later demonstrated when the Western media published proof that the Molotov-Ribbentrop Pact had divided up the country. The Red Army soldiers may not have been the source of as much terror as the Gestapo, but they were certainly responsible for widespread atrocities, especially in Poland. The Institute of National Remembrance (IPN), a commission created to document crimes against the Polish people, estimated that at least 150,000 people, and possibly as many as 500,000, died under Soviet rule in Lwów, quite apart from the numbers killed by the Nazis.

Hundreds of thousands of others were forced to leave their homeland. Western Ukraine had been part of the Polish Republic before the Soviets annexed it. The IPN lists about 320,000 Poles who were forced to move to the Soviet Union, after the occupation. Other historians put the number of Polish refugees much higher, between 700,000 and one million.

Another report of the German-Soviet invasions of Poland came from my cousin David (Dudek) Ladner. In the midst of this chaos, in September 1939, David, who was still a teenager, volunteered for the Fighting Poland (Polska Walcząca, or PW) resistance group and was mobilized towards the eastern front, but the combination of German bombing and raids by thieves left the group in disarray. He kept walking east and found himself in a Jewish shtetl, where he was received hospitably.

The next day, the shtetl was attacked and burned. With his non-Jewish looks and wearing a peasant coat, David was able to blend in among a group of onlookers, soldiers, and Ukrainian peasants, who cheered the sight of the burning synagogue. He then wandered to a larger nearby town, where he came down with a cold, becoming feverish and very ill. Shortly thereafter my father found him, brought him to Lwów, and nursed him to health. It was one of the oddities of wartime that David was able to board with a local family in Lwów and enroll in a Soviet high school there, where he was safe, at least temporarily.

The year after the invasion, in March of 1940, a large number of Polish officers were marched out to the Katyn Forest, near the Western border of Russia, by the NKVD, the Soviet secret police. The number of victims of what is called the Katyn massacre — which includes Polish officers executed in the Khalin and Karkhiv prisons — is estimated to be 22,000. Of this total, 8,000 were officers captured during the Soviet invasion in 1939. About 6,000 were not soldiers but police officers. The remainder were Polish intelligentsia, including landowners, factory owners, lawyers, and even priests. The Soviet Union claimed falsely that the Nazis were responsible for the Katyn massacre. They maintained that lie until April of 1990, when they finally admitted responsibility for the massacre and apologized to the Polish people. Sadly, most of the immediate families of those who were murdered were no longer alive to hear the admission.

So when my father entered the area around Lwów, he faced highly organized persecution on the part of the Soviet Union. As both a soldier and a doctor, he most certainly would have been put to death if he were arrested and his background were revealed. Fortunately, Monek was able to make his way out of the city to the resort town of Truskawiec.

It seems emblematic of who he was that, amidst the horrors of the Second World War, my father somehow found his way to a town known for healing. Truskawiec opened its first mineral baths to visitors in 1827, when the local territory of Galicia was part of the Austrian empire. In 1836, the town's waters were analyzed by Theodore Torosevych, a local chemist and pharmacist better known for the invention of the kerosene lamp. His study confirmed medical properties of the minerals, especially the rare but beneficial ozokerite. After the Austro-Hungarian empire collapsed, Truskawiec became part of Poland from 1920 to 1939, and the development of its healing-waters industry flourished. More than 300 hotels, villas, and guest houses were built to accommodate those who came to Truskawiec for health and medical treatment. The steady stream of visitors ended when the Soviets occupied Galicia in 1939, but some of the resorts still functioned.

Monek managed to find a job as a doctor at a sanatorium. Neither Nazi nor Soviet soldiers bothered him there. In fact, he was able to observe visiting Russians and learn some of their cultural habits and priorities, information that, although he did not yet realize it, would prove useful to him later. He was lucky to find an oasis of peace in the midst of that chaos, but he was still separated from his family, and could get little information about them. My mother and sister, back in Tarnów, knew nothing of his whereabouts.

CHAPTER 3

Ghetto and Gulag

Only a few days after the Germans invaded Poland on September 1, 1939, they took over the town of Tarnów, where many of my family members lived. Tarnów was 45 miles east of Kraków and had a history of resistance. In the First World War, the citizens sided with the Polish fighters, resulting in many battles with the Russian and Austro-Hungarian armies. Tarnów was littered with memorials and graveyards from that war.

On August 28, 1939, German terrorists blew up a bomb in the town's train station, killing 20 and injuring 32. Some historians consider this event the true inciting incident of the Second World War. The bombs began falling on Tarnów six days later, and by September 7, the Nazis had captured the city. Ewa remembers Hela, our mother, looking out the window as the news came in, saying, in German "*So helfe mir Gott*" (so help me God).

The Germans soon established a ghetto for the Jews downtown, into which they crammed more than 40,000 Jews. The Tarnów ghetto had two sections. Section A housed men, women, and children over the age of 12, who were assigned work routines, both inside and outside the ghetto. Its official name was Forced Labor Camp T. Section B was designated for the elderly and the ill, people whom the Germans would soon deport to the camps.

In June of 1942, 728 citizens from Tarnów became the first victims at the infamous camp at Auschwitz. On June 11–13, about 12,000 inhabitants were transported to the Belzec death camp. On September 10, another 8,000 Jews were shipped to Belzec. On November 15, a third Tarnów mass deportation resulted in 3,000 more Jews losing their lives. Many in Section B didn't survive long enough to be put on those trains, dying from starvation and disease or by the whims of their captors.

The Tarnów ghetto included the tailoring shop that my Uncle Ushier Osterweil ran at 7 Lvovska Street. My aunt Hanka Straus-Osterweil, Ushier's wife, gave birth to my cousin Olga in the ghetto. Jews were not allowed to be admitted to hospitals for medical care. Luckily there were no serious complications and both Hanka and Olga were healthy, a great relief to the whole family.

But life in the ghetto was completely unpredictable. Anything could happen at any time, without explanation or discernable logic. Being outside wasn't safe: residents warned each other, for example, of a sadistic SS officer who drove around the ghetto, randomly shooting Jews on the streets. But the Jews were not safe in their apartments either. One day, with neither warning nor explanation, German soldiers pounded on the door, stormed into Hanka and Ushier's apartment, and took away Hanka's grandfather and grandmother, Chaim and Rachel Straus. Hanka's polite protests for information as to where they were being taken were ignored. Her grandparents were taken outside and down a nearby alley. Shots were fired. Hanka never saw her grandparents again. She did not even have the opportunity to learn where they were buried. This was how uncertain life was in the Tarnów ghetto.

Because Hanka and her husband Ushier were still relatively

healthy, they were allowed to live in the A section of the Jewish ghetto and given work documents by the *Judenrat*, the Jewish council that served as intermediary between the Nazis and ghetto residents. This seemed to guarantee Hanka's and Ushier's safety, but only for a while. Again, without explanation, SS officers returned to the apartment. They ordered Hanka and her young son Avram to go downstairs with them to the street, with Ushier and Olga ordered to stay behind. There was no chance to argue. Even asking questions could put one's life in danger.

Outside, Hanka joined a throng of other Jews forced from their homes. One of the SS officers went through the crowd, demanding work permits. Sometimes, he tore up the papers presented to him, without even explaining the reason for doing so. By the time this officer got to Hanka, she was terrified. Fearing that the officer would tear up her work permit, ensuring her doom, Hanka apologized and said she had lost her work permit, even though she had it on her.

The assembled Jews, including Hanka and Avram, were taken in a truck to an outdoor market in the downtown area of Tarnów, where they huddled with other disoriented ghetto residents, waiting for a train. No one would tell them where the train would take them.

After about thirty minutes, a Polish Police officer walked by. Desperate to find a way out of the situation she was caught in, Hanka quickly produced her work permit and asked the officer to help in getting her and my cousin Avram back home. Despite being a Pole, the officer ignored her. Another agonizing thirty minutes crawled by. Hanka saw a German officer walking nearby, she said to him, in German, "I don't know what I'm doing here. I have a work permit." The German officer grabbed the paper from Hanka's hand and studied it for a few moments. "You can go," he said gruffly. "But leave the child here." Then he walked briskly away.

Hanka was stunned. She was sure that leaving her son behind would mean certain death for him. She waited a few moments, then grabbed Avram's hand and dashed away. Hanka was terrified, in those moments, that the crack of a rifle or machine gun would kill them both. Miraculously, however, they ran without being fired upon. Perhaps the German soldiers nearby assumed the officer had told her she and the child could both go.

When Hanka and Avram were a safe distance from the crowd of Jews destined for the trains, they stopped running. They caught their breath and continued walking home, quickly, with Hanka regularly looking back to see if anyone was following them.

My uncle Ushier, even within this nightmarish environment, or perhaps because of it, wanted his son to have more education. He also wanted to keep him occupied to prevent him from getting into trouble on the streets. So Ushier found a *cheder*, a religious class for Jewish children outside of their regular schooling. Though Ushier was a secular man, the *cheder* seemed to be the only available option at the time. My cousin Avram found the *cheder* enjoyable, but for a reason that defeated the purpose his father intended. The aged rabbi who taught the class often fell asleep in front of the students. This provided the children the chance to sneak quietly out of the room and play outside, while the rabbi caught up on his rest.

Feeling that his family might find more safety in a larger city, my uncle Ushier acted on information he heard. The Germans had opened a new textile factory in Kraków. Through his connections in the *Judenrat*, Ushier arranged for the family to move to the ghetto in Kraków. He also found a small apartment they could live in.

There was, however, a small problem with the apartment. They shared it with two women who turned out to be prostitutes. The place was always filled with unknown men, waiting for their services. Avram recalls that he used to roam around among the guests, receiving attention from everyone. There may not have been much privacy and there certainly wasn't much room, but my uncle felt it was safer to live in the Kraków ghetto than in Tarnów.

Not long before this, my mother made the opposite decision. She had been living in Kraków with my sister Ewa, but after Monek was drafted, they moved to Tarnów. Hela's mother, Cywia, was in Tarnów, and they wanted to be close to her. Hela and Ewa joined my grandmother in her spacious apartment on Targowa Street. Unfortunately, Tarnów turned out to be as horrifying for my mother as it had been for my aunt Hanka. One day Germans arrived at the apartment, and my mother exclaimed, "*Helf Got,*" or "God help us," as she and Ewa were forcibly taken downstairs to stand in a courtyard with the other inhabitants.

A German soldier with a flashlight hanging around his neck went into the basement of the building on Targowa Street. He found Cywia and two other elderly women, pulled them out roughly, and forced them to join the others in the courtyard. At this point, little Ewa began to cry, wailing "Grandma, Grandma" over and over.

The German soldier in charge noticed this. He walked over and looked at the elderly women and the crying child. He addressed Hela, indicating the three old women who had been taken from the basement. "Which of these women is related to this beautiful child?" he asked. Ewa had blonde hair, the Aryan model of beauty. The sincerity and intentions of the officer were unclear, but Ewa, being very young and having no understanding of the situation, pointed to her grandmother. The soldier pushed Cywia toward Hela. "Take good care of this old woman," he said, acting as if he had some degree of compassion. Then he grabbed the two older women who had been in the basement and dragged them away. It was yet another incomprehensible incident in Tarnów under Nazi occupation.

The apartment on Targowa Street was outside the confines of the ghetto, so shortly after this incident Cywia, Hela, and Ewa were forced to move into a small, back-alley apartment they had to share with other stunned, displaced Jews. In the ghetto my mother and Ewa spent a great deal of time at the home of Ruzia, my mother's sister, whose husband, Herman, was in the United States, unable to bring his family to join him. Ruzia and Herman had three sons: David, Henek, and the youngest, Fredek. David was the one who had gone to Lwów and been nursed back to health by my father. Henek and Fredek remained in Tarnów.

Because the residents of the Tarnów ghetto were isolated from the rest of the town and the country, they depended all the more on those they knew and trusted for information, for company, and for moral support. Ruzia had more room in her apartment than my mother, so it was there that she and my sister found solace, eating together and letting the children play under their mothers' watchful eyes. Henek, for example, taught little Ewa how to draw. Despite the constant fear, the sisters tried to create some sense of normalcy, but this was nearly impossible in a place where life could end in the blink of an eye. One day, Ruzia and her son Fredek disappeared. According to what we heard, they were shot to death in the street by soldiers. Ruzia's second son, Henek, was taken away to perform forced labor in a camp. His fate is unknown to this day.

Ruzia's eldest son, David, was unaware of his mother and brothers' fates. When he graduated from the Soviet gymnasium in Lwów in the summer of 1940, he registered with the German commission there, because he was told that if he did so he could return to Tarnów. Instead of being sent home, however, he and most of the other people who had registered were sent to the Russian side, where they were consigned to the Soviet gulags. Two older relatives — my mother's brother, Fredek Ladner, and my father's brother, Aron Osterweil — were also in Lwów. As David was still a minor, they figured that if the three of them awaited deportation in one apartment together, they could be shipped to Siberia as a family, where they might have somewhat better conditions than they would as single men.

The ruse worked, and they took a long journey by train, boat, and horse-drawn wagon to a work camp deep in the Siberian taiga, where they were forced to cut and haul trees for the Soviet state timber company. The food, clothing, and medical care they were given was minimal, and the work was dangerous. They were also cut off from any news other than Soviet propaganda, so they had no idea what was happening in the wider world.

After the German invasion of the Soviet Union in June of 1941, however, alliances changed, and Polish prisoners were released from the work camps. They were given papers that allowed them to travel, but they had no money, so my cousin David Ladner and my uncles Fredek Ladner and Aron Osterweil, already malnourished and weak, began an arduous, circuitous journey, stopping in places where they could find work so they could get enough money to continue on. They were not able to return to Poland until the war was over. David was occasionally able to communicate with his father in the United States by mail, but neither of them could get news from Tarnów. They had no way of knowing that things there were continuing to get worse, and that some of their family members were already dead.

CHAPTER 4

Life and Death in the Ghetto

In the Tarnów ghetto, the horror continued.

My mother's sister Rena, who was divorced, kept herself going by devoting herself to her only child, her son Adam. Then, one day, Adam did not return home. Despite the family's best efforts, his whereabouts could not be discovered. They presumed that he was dead. Rena, like so many others, did not even have a grave to visit.

For my mother, one of the worst moments was the day a lone German soldier was roaming from apartment to apartment in her building. When Hela answered the hammering at the door, the soldier, gun at the ready, pushed past her, insisting he was looking for people who were hiding from the Germans. He moved around the apartment until he realized that the only people present were the attractive woman in front of him and her child, busy concentrating on the toy she was playing with in the corner.

The soldier looked at Ewa and then at my mother. He put down his weapon and pushed Hela down on a bed, unzipping his pants. In that moment, my mother realized that if she fought back or cried out, it was more than just her own life at stake. Ewa looked up, confused by the two adults writhing around on a bed nearby. Then she turned her attention back to playing. My mother could only hope that the rape would end quickly and that she could protect her child by remaining silent and cooperating in this most hideous act.

When the soldier was done, he took his gun and left the apartment without a backward glance. Hela took Ewa and went to a friend's apartment nearby. She told the friend what had just happened and asked for advice on how to avoid becoming pregnant.

To my mind, my mother showed great bravery by allowing herself to be humiliated by the soldier, knowing that her daughter could be taken away from her, for any reason, at any moment, and moved to the part of the ghetto where women and children had no work permit. In that area of Tarnów, an *akcja* — an "action" or deportation by the Germans — happened more frequently. If Ewa had lived in that area of the ghetto, her next stop could well have been the death camps at Auschwitz or Belzec.

As far as I know, I was the only other person my mother told this story to. She told me as part of her storytelling sessions, very late in her life. As long as she lived, I kept the story secret. On the day of her funeral, as we were wheeling her body to the grave site, I could not help but share the story with my sister, perhaps to alleviate the burden.

My sister looked at me. "I know," she said. "I was there."

Much of daily life in the Tarnów ghetto consisted of Jewish residents asking each other for information about upcoming raids by the Germans, or news of those who had already been grabbed from their squalid homes. Rampant and often inaccurate guesses and rumors about the next *akcja* only compounded the terror, leading to constant suspicion and worry. My father's brother Herman Osterweil, however, was a relatively reliable source of information, as he was connected to people in the *Judenrat*, and the Germans sometimes shared their plans with *Judenrat* members they knew.

One day Herman Osterweil informed Hela that there was going to be a massive *akcja* in the ghetto. She remembered that my father had told her that if she ever needed help, she should go to the Jewish hospital in Tarnów, where Monek knew the director. So my mother took little Ewa to the hospital and asked if they could stay there until the latest Nazi action had transpired.

The director wanted to help her, but he explained that every person in the hospital, both staff and patients, had to be accounted for. If any person was found hiding there, it would result in the director himself being killed.

My mother was so frightened that she did not go back to the apartment in the ghetto. Ripping off her *opaska* — a white armband about four inches wide with a dark blue Star of David on it, which identified her as a Jew — she went into the area of Tarnów where Jews were forbidden to enter. She intended to walk to the old building where the family used to live, and where a man named Kocik was their veteran, reliable janitor. But she was terrified that if the Germans caught her, they would take Ewa away.

She spotted a gentile young couple holding hands as they walked along an attractive boulevard. Instinctively, she made a choice to approach them. My mother always trusted her intuition, and she simply felt in the moment that this was the right thing to do. She explained that she had to run an errand and was unable to bring Ewa along. Since the couple was walking in that direction, would they kindly bring Ewa to the house of my mother's sister, where the janitor Kocik was overseeing the property? She asked them to explain the matter to Kocik and gave the couple his address and a few *zloty*. She took a huge risk in doing so, assuming that the couple would think her a gentile. Many citizens, if approached by a Jew in hiding, would act very friendly, take their money, and then turn them in to the Gestapo, which paid informers.

Remarkably, the couple agreed to do the favor. After hiding for a while and looking out for soldiers who might be pursuing her, Hela took the chance to walk to her old home. She was nervous that if she met anyone's glance her fear would betray her, so she removed her glasses. Her vision was so poor that without them, she would be unable to see people's faces clearly. She took a roundabout route to the family house.

When she finally got there, Ewa had safely arrived, but Kocik looked very concerned. "Did you know the couple that brought Ewa over here?" he asked her.

"Of course," my mother lied. "Don't worry." Yet even though her gamble paid off, my mother and my sister were by no means out of danger. In the building that Kocik managed there were apartments occupied by Ukrainian *folkdeutsches*, Ukranians of German descent who assisted the German occupiers. Kocik told those nosy enough to ask who Hela was that she was his adopted daughter.

But Kocik could not continue to risk his life by hiding Jews. The longer Hela and Ewa stayed, the greater their chance of being spotted. Eventually, they returned to the tiny apartment in the ghetto. There, however, they soon heard information about another Nazi *akcja,* and they again made their way to Kocik's apartment. This time, Kocik was even more nervous about being discovered, which would mean the execution of all three of them, so he said he was going to go to the countryside to stay with family members until the danger had passed.

Hela asked Kocik to lock her and Ewa in a space on the top floor, under a staircase, where plumbing pipes and electrical wires took up part of the room. There was a sink and toilet and barbed wire running across the window. Kocik hammered boards across the door, preventing anyone from getting in, as well as stopping Hela and Ewa from getting out. He left them with food and water, and pencils and paper, so Ewa could occupy herself with drawing and not make noise. Making art could always keep Ewa's attention, so the drawing kept her quiet. Ewa went on to develop her artistic abilities, especially in the area of painting, even exhibiting her work in galleries. A painting she did, as a child, depicting an *akcja* she witnessed, is today in the Yad Vashem Museum in Jerusalem. (Yad Vashem is Israel's World Holocaust Remembrance Center.)

The space under the staircase was small and dark. Adding to their misery, late at night, was the sound of drunken laughter from the *folkdeutsches* who lived there, whose cackling resonated through the water pipes and woke up Hela and Ewa as they tried to sleep in the cramped hiding space. But they made it through, and when Kocik returned from staying with his relatives in the country, he let them out.

There was no reason or logic as to who survived and who died. Kocik, who helped my mother and sister elude the Nazi raids in Tarnów, helped other Jews as well, but he himself was not as fortunate. Two Jewish women who had left their luggage with Kocik were caught by the Gestapo on the street. When they were searched, Kocik's address was found. He was sent to Auschwitz, where, we assume, he died.

Another man who helped many Jews was Julius Madritsch, who owned a tailoring factory in Tarnów where my uncles Ushier and Herman both worked. He was a Viennese industrialist who wanted to avoid being drafted into the *Wehrmacht*. He had moved to Kraków, and by the end of 1940, had opened two garment-manufacture factories there that had 300 sewing machines for garment manufacture and employed 800 Poles and Jews.

Madritsch became a trustee of the German occupying government. Through coordination with the *Judenrat* in Kraków, and with the help of his factory manager and fellow Austrian, Raimund Titsch, Madritsch's factory provided decent working conditions, plentiful food, and additional bread for Jewish workers to share or sell when they returned to the ghetto. He even created a kosher kitchen for the workers. Only forty percent of the people who worked for Madritsch were professionals. He understood that the more Jews he employed, the better their chances of avoiding annihilation.

Madritsch then opened another factory in Tarnów. A company car for the transportation of textiles was secretly used to smuggle food into the Tarnów ghetto, with the full knowledge of Madritsch and Titsch. Madritsch even helped some workers escape from the Kraków factory and meld into the local population, giving them a chance to flee Poland, usually by way of Slovakia and then Hungary.

Another hero in this story, who helped Madritsch in his attempts to save Kraków Jews, was a ghetto policeman named Oswald Bosko. A police sergeant, Bosko was assigned to guard the Kraków ghetto, even though the rest of his regiment had been sent to the town of Kolomyja, a major transit point on the way to the Belzec death camp. Bosko's associates were part of the directive that reduced Kolomyja's 60,000 Jews to a mere two hundred by the time the War ended.

Bosko and a small number of other compassionate, Vienna-born policemen were responsible for escorting prisoners to and from Madritsch's Kraków factory. The Germans told them to count the prisoners before each leg of the journey, back and forth. When prisoners decided to run, however, these policemen looked the other way, then reported to the German authorities that they had done their head count and all the prisoners were accounted for. As the Germans made plans for the liquidation of the Kraków ghetto, which took place on March 13, 1943, many Jews hid in basements and bunkers, and Bosko saw to it that his sympathetic police associates escorted many of them to the Kraków factory for safety.

Madritsch later wrote about this smuggling operation, which required great effort and courage on the part of those who helped. (His memoir is entitled *Menschen in Not!* or *People in Need!*) "Small children were anesthetized and put in rucksacks," Madritsch wrote, "so that they could not be endangered by crying." He noted that, during the Kraków liquidation, Polish citizens agreed to hide Jewish children in their homes. "Even men from the *Wehrmacht*," Madritsch wrote, "who were heading to Tarnów, took women and children with them." These German soldiers, though few in number, brought many Jewish refugees to Madritsch's Tarnów factory.

Oswald Bosko was remembered by survivor Yaakov Sternberg, who worked in Madritsch's factories and whose written testimony is in the Yad Vashem archive of the Righteous Among the Nations. "Thanks to his straight character and sense," Yaakov wrote of Bosko, "food was brought into the ghetto through all kinds of tricks. Lots of Jews survived, thanks to Bosko, by escaping from the ghetto before deportations. Whenever they felt that something was bound to happen, Bosko made it possible for them to flee to Polish residents."

Unfortunately, even though he provided safety for others, Bosko himself became a victim. As Sternberg testified, "The Gestapo found out about his help to the Jews. Bosko fled but was caught and executed. He was one of the World's Righteous."

Madritsch was by no means completely safe himself, nor seen to be above the law of the Reich. He had to intervene regularly with the SS, local police, and the Labor Office regarding work permits for the Jews he hired. The Labor Office insisted he should hire only Poles, which would have meant certain death for his Jewish employees.

Other government labor employees charged in an official document that Madritsch was "a saboteur of the Jewish transfer [into the ghetto] and could encounter difficulties with the Gestapo."[4]

Later in the war, Madritsch's name was found on a list taken from a captured member of the Polish underground. Madritsch was questioned by the Gestapo and claimed he had no knowledge of the man. He was imprisoned for twelve days. Thanks to his connections, Madritsch was eventually let out and suffered no other punishment from the Nazis.

Madritsch continued his secret advocacy for the Jews in Kraków and Tarnów, using the most effective excuse he had, that the Jewish workers were "important for the war effort." He befriended Oskar Schindler, commemorated in the book and film *Schindler's List*, who also saved as many Jews as he could by employing them. One of the reasons Madritsch was able to operate without obstruction was because of his strong relationships with SS men, including the infamous Amon Goeth, the cruel commandant at the Płaszów slave labor camp, who had to be bribed regularly. The record also shows that a German lieutenant colonel named Mathisen helped certain Jews escape via Madritsch's factory.

Madritsch and Schindler even attended a *Judenrat* conference together, to try to keep up with the constantly changing rules of the German occupation. Jews were only allowed to work in armaments factories and only for a limited time. Madritsch and Schindler managed to have their factories reclassified under the category of armaments, since German uniforms were being manufactured there. The Armament Inspectorate, as it was called, provided legal protection,

---

4   Julius Madritsch file M.31.2/21, The Righteous Among the Nations Database, Yad Vashem.

however briefly, for the Jews who worked for Madritsch and Schindler. One of the many people who helped make this possible was a man named Franz Fritsch. As shop director in Tarnów, Fritsch had permission to travel all over Poland to purchase materials for Madritsch's factories. Fritsch was also known for his bravery in support of Jewish workers. A handsome, single man with an outgoing personality, Fritsch managed to make deals with the Nazis on behalf of Madritsch.

On one occasion, Fritsch went to the Gestapo in Tarnów and asked to have Jewish workers taken off the list of those who would be put on trains and taken to their deaths. The official he dealt with agreed and made a list of fifty Jewish workers. Fritsch doctored this official-looking list so that it eventually numbered 250, saving an additional 200 lives.

One of the Jews that Madritsch saved in this manner was my uncle Herman Osterweil, who had connections with the *Judenrat* and worked in Madritsch's factory. Before the Nazis invaded, Uncle Herman had lived with my aunt Faiga and my cousin Jerzyk in a relatively modern building at 12 Piłsudkiego Street, not far from Strzelecki Park. Herman's previous work had been in metallurgy, employed by his uncle. Later he and a partner established a factory for the manufacture of men's shirts, a company called OPE, but it was taken away by the Germans.

When Herman and his family were forced to enter the Tarnów ghetto, they moved into a small apartment on Wałova Street that was shared with another family. The only separation between the two families in the one-room apartment was a blanket that served as a curtain, for minimal privacy.

While Herman, along with his brother Ushier, worked in Madritsch's Tarnów factory, Faiga remained at home with Jerzyk and tried to protect him as best as she could. During each *akcja*, the children saw regular roll calls of Jews by the Germans in the nearby market plaza, Rynek, also called Świnski Plac or "the pork market." There, under armed guard, Jews were chosen for deportation. There were so many shootings on the streets of the ghetto that the citizens developed a slang word for them, *kałuża* or "small pool," suggesting a pool of blood from a shooting victim. In typical fashion, the children found a way to cope with the grim reality by incorporating the horrors of daily life into the games they played in the courtyards of their buildings. At the building where Jerzyk lived, it was common for the children to play as Germans and Jews. The children who played the Germans would line up the children who took on the role of the Jews and then one group would pretend to shoot down the other, just as they had tragically witnessed in their daily lives in the ghetto.

CHAPTER 5

Forced Labor in Janowska

My father never told me exactly what made him leave the relative safety of Truskawiec. It may have been that his identity as a Jew was going to put him in jeopardy and that he feared for his wellbeing. Probably it was primarily that he longed for his family and needed to know if they were still alive. Whatever the reasons, he left the resort town and headed back toward Lwów, where so many Polish officers and Jewish professionals had been rounded up by the Russians. Now the Nazis had taken over. In 1941, the area, including Truskawiec, was taken over by the Germans.

In August, 1939, as I have related, the Soviet Union had made a deal to join Germany and divide the spoils of war. In June, 1941, for their acquiescence, the Soviets were rewarded with Germany's sudden attack on Russian-held Lwów, an early part of the German offensive known as Operation Barbarossa. An estimated three million German soldiers attacked Soviet-held territory in eastern Galicia, the largest number of men in a war campaign in the history of the world. The intent was to remake the western Soviet Union into a German territory, use the captured as slave labor, and take advantage of the oil deposits in the Caucasus and agricultural production of that area of the Soviet Union.

The irony of the USSR trusting Germany is that the Soviets were treated in much the same way as both countries treated the Jews in Poland. The five million Red Army soldiers captured by the Germans were not provided the protections due according to the Geneva Conventions. The Germans starved to death or otherwise killed 3.3 million Russian soldiers, as well as many civilians, through the "Hunger Plan" that attempted to turn USSR territory into German satellites. All told, the Soviet Union would lose 26 million of its own people, a statistic of almost unimaginable horror.

The Nazis, of course, treated Soviet Jewry with the same barbarity. Nazi death squads or the SS *Einsatzgruppen* murdered about one million Russian Jews. German soldiers were often involved in the gang-raping of Soviet women; if the female victim was Jewish, more likely than not she was shot afterward.

When my father left Truskawiec, he made it no farther than Lwów. By the end of 1941, he was captured by Germans and sent to the infamous Janowska camp, which served as a location for forced labor, transit, and later, murder. The camp, at 134 Janowska Street in the southwest outskirts of Lwów, had been set up in September of 1941 as the German Armament Works (known as the DAW in German), part of a chain of factories in occupied Poland. In October, the factory, which had employed about six hundred carpenters and metalworkers, was converted to a labor camp. Smaller branches of Janowska were set up in neighboring towns such as Laski Kurowice, Jaktarowe and others, where Jewish slave laborers were sometimes transferred. In November, the Nazis asked the head of the Lwów *Judenrat*, Dr. Joseph Parnes, to provide more Jewish workers for the camp. Heroically, he refused, and was shot.

The main camp was divided into three sections. The first section contained garages, workshops, and offices, with accommodations for staff. At the center of this first section was the villa for the camp commandant. The second section was the armaments factory. The third section was the main reason for the camp: forced labor.[5] It was this third section that my father became most familiar with.

Here Jews who were not immediately killed because of age or illness were assigned to work details, groups of twenty to thirty people who were worked twelve hours a day. Some of the men were assigned to burying the Jewish dead, particularly those executed on the Piaski sand hills behind Janowska. Others were put to work sorting the clothing and possessions of the recently killed. Monek was assigned to the local Jewish cemetery in Lwów, where, under supervision of Ukrainian and German guards, he and other Jews were put to work smashing the headstones of the Jewish dead into rubble, to be used for paving roads in the area.

For Monek and other work-crew prisoners, the days began with a coffee substitute (*ersatzkaffee*). Prior to going out with his crew to the cemetery each day, Monek had to answer a roll call. An SS officer inspected each worker before he went out to smash grave markers. Any prisoner who did not pass inspection was shot.

The food the prisoners received was just enough to starve them within weeks or months. At midday workers received a watery soup with unpeeled potatoes. At the end of a long day of labor, they received pieces of bread weighing no more than 200 grams (seven ounces). The barracks where they slept housed two thousand prisoners each, in horrifying conditions. Prisoners slept on the ground

---

5   For more information on the Janowska camp, see for example Okeksandr Pahiria, "The Janowska concentration camp: What we know and don't know," July 31, 2020, Ukrainian Jewish Encounter. https://ukrainianjewishencounter.org/en/the-janowska-concentration-camp-what-we-know-and-dont-know/, retrieved 11/11/2021.

or on rough wooden planks. Sanitation was crude and so, in addition to deaths by starvation, many died due to outbreaks of disease.

After each exhausting day, my father and his coworkers were escorted by armed men back to Janowska, and when they arrived at the gates, they were forced to run into the camp. Those who were not able to do so were taken aside by one of the commanders, Gustav Wilhaus, and his assistant. These exhausted men were left outside, where they would die.

Escape from Janowska seemed possible. True, each section of Janowska was separated by barbed wire, and the perimeter of the camp had a double barbed wire fence, illuminated by searchlights. Guard dogs were stationed every fifty meters, and armed Ukrainian guards and SS men provided even more security over the victims. The camp was guarded by a shift of twelve to fifteen guards at a time, and these were replaced regularly.

But the back of the camp, facing the Piaski sand hills, was unfenced, tempting some inmates to try to escape. Most were caught and returned, then shot to teach others a lesson. Nor were the escapees the only ones to suffer. The prisoners were told that for anyone who attempted escape, nine others in their barracks would be shot. This resulting atmosphere of terror led to the inmates watching their own peers and preventing their escape.

The permission to kill at will in Janowska brought out the full range of Nazi depravity. Shooting was the most humane form of execution: at least the victim did not suffer long. Part of the torment was how arbitrarily death came. Monek and the other prisoners soon learned that you could be executed on the spot, not just for being injured or ill but for any reason, or for no discernible reason at all. Maybe you took too long to respond to an order. Maybe you moved too slowly. Maybe the officer was in a bad mood, or didn't like your expression, or you reminded him of someone he did not like. One officer, Wilhelm Rokita, had a habit of casually passing by the prisoners in the parade ground in Janowska. If he saw a prisoner he simply did not like the looks of, he casually pulled out his gun and shot the man in the back of the head. There were no rules, no ethics, no control.

Execution methods were not confined to bullets. Janowska survivors recalled witnessing execution by flogging, hanging, choking, crucifying with the head pointed down to the ground, and cutting victims to pieces with knives or axes. The Jewish women were primarily executed through flogging or stabbing. Various SS men had their own favorite methods. Janowska commandant Fritz Gebauer often spontaneously choked a prisoner to death. Rokita was known to cut open the stomachs of his victims. The chief of Janowska's investigation department, a man called Heine, was seen stabbing people with iron rods or spikes. He pulled out the fingernails of Jewish women, hung them from poles by their hair, and, as their bodies swung from side to side, used them for target practice.

The Nazis even conducted some acts of brutality to music. At Janowska, a prisoner orchestra was assembled from musicians in Lwów. They played a piece that some Jewish prisoners composed, called "The Death Tango," on command. Those who left the camp in the morning to go to work assignments were ordered to sing and even make up songs, for the pleasure of the Germans who supervised them.

Not all prisoners of the camp were treated equally. Janowska was originally set up for Jews, but after a couple of months, Poles and Ukrainians were also sent there. The Germans viewed Polish and Ukrainian Galicians, who had lived in the former Austro-Hungarian Empire, as closer to their Aryan ideal. These prisoners were housed separately from Jews, treated much better, and eventually released. In March of 1942, Janowska took on an additional function. In addition to being a forced labor camp, it also now became a transit camp, where Jews from the surrounding towns and villages were kept until it was decided whether to kill them on the spot, use them for labor, or deport them to death camps. That same month, March of 1942, Janowska became a transfer point for Jews to be murdered in the camp known as Belzec, located on the railway line that connected Lublin to Lwów.

Belzec was built specifically as a death camp. The gas chambers there were rudimentary at first, housed in leaky wooden buildings. Later in the year, the process of killing was refined there, including the development of Zyklon B, the gas that at first was used for delousing and later became an agent of slaughter.

Unlike at Janowska, at Belzec the Nazis made an attempt to pacify and delude the arrivals. Christian Wirth, Belzec's infamous first commandant, was known by other SS men as "Savage Christian." His was the first voice Jews heard over loudspeakers as they were taken off the trains. His usual welcoming speech was this: "This is Belzec. Your stay is temporary. You will move onto work camps where your skills are needed. There is work for everyone. Even you housewives are needed to feed your families and keep the houses clean. First, I must have your cooperation so that we can get you on your way quickly." Survivors of Belzec recalled how sometimes there was a ripple of relieved applause and even shouted thanks from new arrivals, even though it was all lies to make the butchery more efficient. Then, completing this deception, Wirth would announce, "We must have order and cleanliness. Before we feed you, you must all have a bath and have your clothes disinfected. It is necessary for the women to have their hair cut." Belzec was about speed. Those arrivals who protested or were ill were taken to burial pits and shot and the rest were gassed immediately after.

By May of 1942, back at Janowska, Gustav Wilhaus, the former deputy commandant, was given complete command. His superior, Gebauer, the first commandant of the camp, was now in charge of the DAW, the armaments factory. Wilhaus was just as mentally disturbed as his predecessor. In 1943, Monek and other prisoners at Janowska, started witnessing a new horror. Wilhaus, to amuse himself, his wife, and his young daughter, would on occasion fire a machine gun from the balcony of his camp office into a workshop filled with prisoners. Then he would pass the weapon to his wife, who would do the same.

My father miraculously survived these horrors at Janowska, but on at least two occasions he came very close to becoming incapacitated, which almost certainly would have led to his execution. One day, during work detail, a soldier decided that my father was not working fast enough at breaking up the headstones at the Jewish cemetery. In anger, the soldier struck my father on the head with the handle of his pistol. The injury created internal bleeding, eventually leading to a partial loss of vision in one of his eyes, but Monek still managed to get up each day and work his twelve hours, keeping himself alive.

Besides his iron will, one thing that helped my father stay alive in Janowska was his medical knowledge. One of the female guards knew, probably from the camp's physician, that Monek had been a pediatrician before he was captured. She approached him and confided, "I have a daughter who's been sick with a fever and a rash for more than a week. She's not eating or drinking and has a sore throat. There are complications. I need your help."

Monek saw the child and diagnosed her with measles. He assumed that due to the sickness, she had become severely dehydrated. He advised the guard to feed the child borscht and cooked potatoes, the food the woman had available. The guard followed his advice. With better hydration, her daughter eventually regained her strength, overcame the illness, and recovered fully. The guard gave my father additional food to thank him for his help.

On another day, Moneky found that he simply could not get up for work detail, though he knew what would happen if he didn't rise. He had contracted typhus, a disease born by insects and other parasites that infects the bloodstream when the victim scratches the insect bite. Today it is easily treated by antibiotics and is rare where modern hygiene prevails. In conditions of squalor and without treatment, however, the disease can progress from fever, chills, severe headaches, and muscle aches to a rash, coughing, nausea, stomach pain, vomiting, loss of appetite and confusion, with subjects often seeming out of touch with reality. The camp doctor came to see my father and urged him to get up and go to work. Monek was unable to move. The doctor kicked my father's feet. "If you wish to live," he shouted, "get up and go to work!"

Though Monek couldn't get up, the doctor nevertheless contrived to keep him alive, so he could make use of Monek's medical knowledge. This came in handy when the commandant's nine-year-old daughter, too, contracted measles. As it worsened, encephalitis with seizures set in. My father gave the camp doctor medical advice, which was passed on to Commandant Wilhaus, and the child's life was saved.

One of the most repugnant memories of Janowska was the time that Wilhaus, to please his nine-year-old daughter, had a soldier toss two four-year-old children into the air, while he fired upon them. His daughter shouted out with glee, "*Wunderbar*, Papa, do it again!

Papa, do it again!" This, in one of the ironies of war, was the child that had been saved by my father. Though his own life was spared as a result, he had to live with the knowledge of saving a child who was, unfortunately, a monster like her father.

My father saw many horrors at Janowska, but, as I have related earlier, one particular event changed his life. After another long day of being forced to smash the gravestones of his people, he rounded a corner near the bathrooms and saw camp guards forming a firing squad to mow down a row of small children with their machine guns. As he hid behind the outhouses, he saw the faces of the terrified children, he saw the men raise their guns, and he watched as those small bodies were perforated by bullets. At that moment, he decided there was no such thing as God. No Creator, he felt, would allow such horrific taking of life. No divine guide would allow the soldiers to perform such an unforgivable act.

Years later, my sister Ewa shared with me that my father had once told her about that same incident. He had added one important detail: Though he lost any semblance of religious faith to help him get through Janowska, my father made a vow when he saw those children murdered: if he managed to survive the camp and the war, he pledged to himself to dedicate at least one year of his life to rescue and care for children in need. His determination to fulfill that vow may very well have provided him the drive he needed to survive.

Figure 1: Ewa Osterweil. Tarnów

Figure 2: Ladner Family in Borek, Poland, my mother's birthplace.
Hela is seated in the second row, right. Her mother, Cywia
(Munderer) Ladner, is in the middle of third row. Hela's brother
Herman Ladner is in the back row, second from left, with flowers.

Figure 3: My maternal grandfather, Leon Ladner

Figure 4: Hela Ladner-Osterweil, Tarnów

Figure 5: My paternal grandfather, Jakub Izrael Osterweil (with Panama hat), in his Tarnów workshop, 1906

Figure 6: Monek (Moshe) Osterweil, Tarnów, 1929

Figure 7: Meeting of the local chapter of HaShomer Hatzair, Tarnów. From left: Monek Osterweil, Monek Grinstein, unknown, Sala Ladner, Hela Ladner, Kuba Fleischer.

Figure 8: Fredrick Ladner (Fredek)

Figure 9: My maternal grandmother, Cywia (Munderer) Ladner and Hela Ladner

Figure 10: The Ladner Sisters: Sala, Ruzia, Regina (aka Rena) and Helena (Hela)

Figure 11: Ewa and Jerzyk, 1941

Figure 12: Faiga and Herman Osterweil

Figure 13: Jerzyk , 1938. Inscription reads "To aunt Hela from Jerzyk, many kisses with his own handwritten signature." This photo was sent to an aunt in Palestine and thus survived.

Figure 14: Akcja in the Ghetto, by Ewa Osterweil, 1977.
Original at Yadvashem, Jerusalem

PART TWO: ESCAPE

CHAPTER 6

Fritsch's Plan

My uncle Ushier was working as usual in Julius Madritsch's garment factory in Tarnów when the shop director, Franz Fritsch, approached him with a quiet question. "Have you thought about escaping from here?" Unsure how to react, Ushier just stared at him. "If you stay," Fritsch continued, "you will all very likely be killed." Ushier still gave no response. "I have it all figured out in my head," Fritsch said, and began to explain his plan, with Ushier listening cautiously.

He would need the equivalent of a few thousand dollars, Fritsch said, to carry out his plan. It was a lot of money. Ushier knew that Fritsch had helped other Jews, but Ushier didn't know if he could be completely sure of this man, and trusting the wrong person in those times could be fatal. He asked for a few days to consider the proposal. Fritsch agreed to wait for Ushier's reply. He warned my uncle to be careful about discussing the plan with anyone but said Ushier could invite other people he trusted to join the group, if they had the necessary money.

One of the few people Ushier discussed the idea with was my mother. She had already spoken to a number of Polish underground operatives who were reputed to have smuggled Jews out of the country. They had told her that my father was rumored to be in the labor camp at Janowska, but she had no way to confirm that information. Though she was aware of the growing danger of remaining in the ghetto, she couldn't bring herself to trust any of these men, with their long sideburns and dirty fingernails. She later said, "They reminded me of street thugs, like plain criminals." Her impression of Fritsch was better, so she was willing to consider his offer.

Ushier brought Fritsch to Hela's apartment, where he presented his plan. Fritsch acknowledged that he was asking for a lot of money, but he insisted that it was necessary. He was convinced that Monek was indeed in the Janowska camp, and his plan now had two parts. In addition to helping Hela, Ewa, Ushier and others escape the Tarnów ghetto, he would also get Monek out of Janowska, and get them all through Slovakia to Hungary. He would have to pay a wide variety of people, including drivers and farmers who would hide and feed them along the way. By the end of the meeting, Hela was convinced this was the best chance for her and her family. She agreed to pay to get Monek out of Janowska. Ushier would pay for the escape from the ghetto.

These plans were being finalized when Ewa's fifth birthday arrived, on May 6, 1943. There was no party. No childhood friends came over to play with her. Jews in the ghetto could not purchase much beyond the absolute necessities for survival. All that Hela could manage was to throw open the curtains that looked out on the inner courtyard of their building, letting in some light, and to put a nice tablecloth with a floral design on the round table that dominated their one-room apartment. The tablecloth had been one of the few things Hela had been able to bring with them into the ghetto. It reminded Ewa of home, and she found it soothing, as she did her toy bear.

Ewa had asked for a flower for her birthday, and my mother managed to find a single branch of a lilac, which became a symbol in our family. My father, years later, planted a lilac bush under Ewa's window in our garden at the house in Israel. Every year in the spring, around the time of Ewa's birthday, the lilac would bloom and spread its pleasant scent.

Meanwhile, in Tarnów, Ushier needed to find others to contribute money and participate in the secret plan. He approached a friend, Nathan Nudel, who had owned a jewelry shop before it was confiscated by the Nazis. Nathan and his wife were willing to be a part of the potential escape, but Nathan protested that it was too much money. Ushier convinced him by repeating what Fritsch had said about all the people who had to be paid off. Nathan agreed to contribute money so that he and his wife could flee with the others.

Ushier also approached his brother Herman, who worked in the same factory, and who had so many connections and good sources of information, to join the group. Though his wife Faiga's father and sister had already been taken by the Nazis, Herman decided not to go with Ushier and my mother and the Nudels. Perhaps he thought he could find a better or easier way. Perhaps he thought his good connections would be enough to save him and his family even if they stayed. In any case, he passed up this chance for escape. Herman, Faiga, and their son Jerzyk stayed in Tarnów, while my mother, my sister, and my uncle Ushier and his family decided to trust Franz Fritsch and attempt escape.

My father, in Janowska, was unaware of these plans. He had no communication with my mother in the Tarnów ghetto. He continued his daily labor, being driven from Janowska with the other prisoners to the Jewish cemetery to smash gravestones with sledgehammers and reduce them to gravel for paving roads. It therefore came as a complete surprise to him when a man visited the Jewish cemetery, gave the German guard a package of cigarettes, and approached Monek to talk with him privately. The man was Franz Fritsch, who introduced himself in a whisper to my astonished father and told him that my mother and Ushier had arranged for his escape. The escape, Fritsch told my father in hushed tones, would take place the following day.

Hela, Fritsch explained, had already given him half the money necessary to pay those involved in the escape operation. She had agreed to give him the other half of the money only after Monek sent a message from Slovakia to indicate that he was safe. Later, my mother, sister, and others would join him, in a second wave. This second part of the escape was to be financed by Ushier and the others. Monek would therefore be like a scout going ahead of the troops, like a reconnaissance mission to ensure the escape route was safe enough for the rest to follow. So, while Ushier contributed the original initiative and funds, Monek risked his life to ensure they would all be safe.

Monek was impressed by the many details Fritsch knew about his family. He asked how the escape would be organized. "Tomorrow morning," Fritsch said in a low voice, "when they drive you to the cemetery, the truck will, as it usually does, slow down as it gets to the railroad crossing. That's when you jump out. I'll be waiting for you with fresh clothes. Then, we'll take the train to Tarnów." Eventually, Fritsch went on to explain, Monek would be taken south to cross into Slovakia. Assuming Monek was not caught or turned in by Nazi collaborators posing as helpful smugglers, he would then send a prearranged message back to Hela.

My father agreed to the plan and went back that night as usual to his barracks at Janowska. When morning came, he boarded the truck and brought a heavy blanket, which would help protect him from the impact if he fell, leaping from the truck. The guard evidently saw nothing unusual in the blanket, as Monek was still recovering from typhus.

As he sat in the moving truck with two fellow prisoners, however, my father had a difficult choice to make, one he and Fritsch had not discussed. The Germans had made clear that no prisoner would escape from Janowska without reprisals. For each person who escaped, no matter the outcome, nine other prisoners from the same barracks would be shot. Most of the Lwów countryside near the cemetery was inhabited by German sympathizers: even without taking reprisals into account, the odds of escape were not good.

Fear of reprisals among the camp inmates freed the Germans from attaching much security to the trucks that took the prisoners to their outside work assignments. A single guard sat in the cab of the truck next to the driver. In the back, my father sat, wrapped in his blanket and his thoughts. Two younger Jewish prisoners sat with him. A canvas flap preventing them from seeing outside the truck, but they were otherwise unguarded. My father felt he owed those two men the chance to escape with him. He explained the plan. "I have a contact waiting for me," he explained. "He will help you escape as well."

But Monek was still emaciated and weak from the typhus he had contracted. Though still only about 40 years old, he must have been pale and thin, barely getting through his workday in his weakened state. No doubt he looked even more pathetic hunched over and wrapped in his blanket. The two young men thought he was delirious. "You're delusional, old man," said one contemptuously. "The typhus has gone to your head," said the other.

"Trust me," my father begged them. "I'm telling you the truth.

Please join me." He did not want the others to suffer because of his arranged escape, but there was no convincing them. The two prisoners dismissed his pleas as the ravings of a sick and probably dying man. They were stunned when, as the truck slowed as usual for the railroad crossing, my father pushed through the canvas covering the back, climbed over the rear gate of the truck, leaped off the bumper and rolled into the road.

True to his word, Fritsch was waiting for him at the crossing. He pulled my father into an alley, where he gave him a hat, to help cover his face, and new clothes. They walked as quickly as Monek could manage to the local train station. They bought tickets and sat on the train for Tarnów, which was just over 155 miles away. The riders were mostly local farmers and German soldiers. Some of the soldiers were smoking and chatting, on their way home on leave. Others had been injured at the Russian front and wore bandages or casts. Monek tried not to look around at the other passengers and draw attention to himself.

The trip normally took four and a half hours, but the war extended the journey due to added stops or obstructions found on the tracks. The long trip amid many armed Nazis only increased the tension experienced by Monek and Fritsch, but nothing could be done. When they finally arrived at a safe house in Tarnów, Fritsch could see clearly that my father was in no condition to journey immediately to Slovakia. The typhus had drained his energy, and he could not walk for long periods of time.

Fritsch went to see my mother in the ghetto and told her that my father was hiding in a nearby residence and that he was in poor health. Hela was both excited and nervous. She left my sister with a neighbor and went with Fritsch to the safe house.

My mother was thrilled to be reunited with her husband, but the times made their reunion less than completely joyous. He was of course glad to see his wife again, but he had not seen his daughter in four years. "Why didn't you bring Ewa?" he demanded. Hela explained that children were not allowed in that area of town. Bringing her would have put them all in jeopardy.

Additional tension emerged later, when my father learned that another man, a physician, had been visiting Hela. He knew that my father was at Janowska, and that the odds did not favor his survival. My mother was a good-looking woman, and this man was hoping to be part of her life. Ewa recalls that she actually became fond of the man, who acted as a sort of stand-in father to the little girl. My father never asked for more details. Neither he nor I ever learned if my mother had been physically intimate with the man who had been pursuing her in the Tarnów ghetto.

For now, they had to discuss Monek's next move. Going secretly into the ghetto to be with Hela and Ewa was a dangerous proposition. It would put all three of them at risk, as well as Fritsch and perhaps many other people. So Monek's initial reunion with Hela lasted only a few hours.

The next day, Fritsch picked him up in a truck used by Madritsch's factory to transport materials. My father hid under piles of wooden heels to be used for the construction of shoes. He lay buried under the wood for hours, until the truck reached a Polish village near the Slovakian border and went to the house of a Polish farmer. The owner had been paid in advance and was told that Monek was a Polish officer, returning from the eastern front, who needed to rest and recuperate. It was a good cover story, as many soldiers, both Russian and German, contracted diseases or simply lost weight because of stress and lack of food. Medical science now treats typhus with a complete success rate with antibiotics, but vast numbers of those who contracted it during the Second World War died. Spread by lice, typhus became not just a problem in prisons and in the concentration camps, like Janowska, but also amongst armies that had no hygienic controls. During the War, three million men died on the Russian front of typhus. Thus, the Polish farmer who took care of my father readily accepted that Monek had become ill fighting the Russians. Fritsch shook hands with the farmer and my father and promised to be back in about two weeks to check on him.

My father went into a dream world, sleeping almost around the clock, waking up only to take meals from the farmer and his wife. He did not see another person and did not leave the small house. After sixteen days of nothing but sleep and food for my father, Fritsch returned and told the farmer it was time for Monek to return to the front. In reality, my father and Fritsch found a way across the border into Slovakia on foot, evading the authorities. Of course, my father had no passport or other papers, so this was the only way to get to the next safe house.

From the safety of his new location, my father, on a piece of newspaper, wrote a one-sentence note for Fritsch to take back to Tarnów. It was the message Monek and my mother had agreed upon to indicate that he had arrived safely: *"The labor was difficult, but the baby is alive."*

CHAPTER 7

Escaping the Tarnów Ghetto

My mother was not at the apartment when Fritsch arrived, so he handed the handwritten note to my aunt Hanka, Ushier's wife, who promised to give it to Hela. When my mother read the words "the labor was difficult, but the baby is alive" scrawled on that torn piece of newspaper, she knew her husband was out of Poland and that Fritsch could be trusted.

It was growing more and more apparent that they had to make their escape as soon as possible. Despite the additional bread that Madritsch gave his workers to provide for their families and friends in the ghetto, conditions were getting worse. The shortage of food was now life-threatening. Fears of another deportation loomed.

The plan was to follow the same route Monek had taken and then join up with him in Slovakia. On another visit to Hela's apartment, Fritsch told her to take only a bag with a few important belongings for herself and Ewa and to be ready for him later that evening. Hela even left behind Ewa's beloved bear. "We'll come back later and get it for you," she told Ewa. Hela was careful not to discuss the real reasons for their hurried packing, for fear her chatty daughter might discuss it with neighbors.

That evening Fritsch approached a guard patrolling the ghetto perimeter and put him at ease by offering him a cigarette. When the guard was out of sight, Fritsch entered the ghetto through a side door, as prearranged. Hela and Ewa were waiting in a boarded-up former store nearby. Fritsch led them to the door and looked out carefully. The guard was a half block away, continuing his patrol. Fritsch waited until the guard passed them and was walking in the other direction, up the block. Then Fritsch, my mother, and my sister dashed across the street to a military truck that was waiting for them. Fritsch opened the passenger side door and helped my mother and sister into the cab of the truck. Because they were both blonde and therefore Aryan in appearance, he felt it was safe to have them sit where they were visible, at least for a while.

Fritsch hurried to the back of the truck. It was a two-tiered space. As it had been with Monek, the space was filled with wood pieces to be used for making shoes. Hiding under the wood were my uncle Ushier, my aunt Hanka, and their children, Avram, ten, and little Olga, only one year old. They were huddled together with Nathan Nudel, the jeweler, and his wife, who had contributed money as well to be part of the escape.

Ushier and Hanka had gotten Olga out of the ghetto earlier in the day. Because she was too young to keep silent on command, the girl was sedated, put in a backpack, and carried out by a friend, who brought the unconscious Olga to the Madritsch factory in Tarnów. Ushier, Hanka and Avram, who had arrived at the factory earlier, stayed in hiding there until it closed. Then, they all hid in the truck and Fritsch picked up Hela, Ewa, and the Nudels.

The driver was himself a victim of the Nazis, having escaped from the Dachau concentration camp, but he was not Jewish: He had been thrown into the camp because of his political views. Most likely, he was a Communist.

The truck traveled all night. They stopped many times at military roadblocks. German soldiers demanded papers and dogs barked, straining at their leashes, suggesting that they would be discovered. But when the soldiers looked in the back of the truck, all they saw were pieces of wood, and they gave the okay for the truck to proceed.

At dawn, the truck arrived at a small farm in the countryside. The escapees got out, and Fritsch and the farmer directed them to a barn that housed a number of cows. The farmer told my family and the others to hide atop a large haystack. He ordered them not even to talk during the day, so that they would not be discovered by neighbors or people passing by.

The driver, having been paid for his bravery, drove off to abandon the truck. They were now ready to continue on foot, as my father had, across the border, but Fritsch surprised them all by saying he wanted to take a different, shorter route. The shorter the trip, he said, the faster the group would get to safety. This made sense: Ewa had contracted meningitis in the ghetto and was very weak. A shorter trip would help her.

Once again, however, my mother insisted on trusting her intuition. She had a strong feeling that something would go wrong if they took the new route. She could not prove it, and others tried to convince her that it made sense to walk for a shorter time, but she insisted. Her husband had already proven that the path he took was safe, she said, and their group had more people traveling, which would draw more suspicion if they were seen. She succeeded in convincing the others.

The next night, two border smugglers with guns arrived at the barn to lead them to Slovakia. They walked at night through forests and fields and hid and slept during the day. Their night journeys had little light. The children, Avram and Ewa, entertained themselves during the journey by counting the number of glow worms they spotted on the ground.

Though Ewa behaved well, her health began to pose a problem: the meningitis so weakened her that after a while she could no longer walk. Fritsch picked her up and carried her in his arms. Ewa vomited at times, but Fritsch cleaned them both off with his handkerchief, acting as if it were completely normal, and the nightly pilgrimage continued. Hela, grateful for his gallant behavior, gave Fritsch a silver pen she had in her possession.

One morning, they arrived in a village and approached a farmhouse that had a small bowling green in front. They walked in after being out in the cold all night. The farmer asked his daughters to get out of bed and let the guests use them. Little Ewa would remember this moment of bliss, thawing her freezing feet in a bed still warm from the bodies of the girls.

Though Fritsch had seemingly done everything in his power to help my family and the Nudels to escape, including accompanying them himself, he came under suspicion as the group progressed. At one stop along the way, Fritsch announced to Hanka that he had to leave them at that point of the trip, because he was needed back at the factory in Tarnów for work duties. He asked for the rest of the money, which was due upon their safe arrival in Hungary. He was supposed to deliver Hela and Ewa to Monek in Slovakia but had made arrangements to accompany Ushier and his family the whole way through to Hungary.

Hanka, who was a very stoic, serious, and strong-willed woman, let Fritsch know immediately and firmly that the idea was totally unacceptable. "That's out of the question," she answered. "I don't trust these smugglers. Without you here, they might rob us, and we'd never get to Hungary." Fritsch backed down and continued with them.

In the next village they hid in, the fear of discovery loomed again. Close to the border now, almost to their destination, they all heard the sounds of gunfire and dogs barking in the distance. They assumed that German patrols were trying to catch others trying to cross the border, which made them all even more nervous about their own upcoming attempt.

Baby Olga was awakened by the noises and began to cry. Entering the room where she had been sleeping with Hanka and little Olga, Hela saw Ushier putting a pillow near Olga's face to muffle the sound of her cries. "What are you doing?" Hela demanded in a hoarse whisper. "You're suffocating her! You went all this way to save her, only to kill her now?"

Ushier turned to my mother and spoke with emotion. "Everyone shouldn't die because of one child."

The noises faded in the distance and Olga went back to sleep.

The next day, the group made it to the Polish-Slovakian border, where they were met as arranged by two members of the mountain police. There were feathers in their tall helmets, not unlike the Swiss guards in the Alps. The policemen warned the group not to speak, as that might draw the attention of the other guards. How terrible it would be to get this close only to make a careless mistake! They rode the bus together to a nearby small town and arrived at a building where they finally met Monek.

Too soon, they were asked to separate, men in one group, women in the other. At this, the pressure and tension rose sharply. Monek, who had not seen Ewa for four years, wanted her to join him in the men's section. Ewa, who hardly recognized her father, refused. My father, frustrated that she would defy his command when circumstances required quick action, administered the first and only spanking Ewa ever received from him. Hanka, too, panicked, demanding to stay with Ushier. This threatened to draw attention and to expose all of them. My mother took her aside to find out why she was so upset and to try and calm her down. Hanka, breathing heavily, stunned Hela by explaining she had hidden some family diamonds in a tube of toothpaste and had other valuables were tucked away. (Ushier and Hanka were quite well-to-do.) The separation of the sexes, she feared, was to body-search the refugees. If she were searched, Hanka, feared, they would find everything, take it away, and ruin their chances for getting to Hungary and freedom. To her, the hidden valuables meant the difference between safety and despair.

This was a reasonable concern. The little group did not know exactly what awaited them when they got to the Slovakian border. But my mother managed to convince Hanka that, despite the separation, all they would be subjected to at the border would be some standard questions. Thankfully, Hela was right. There was no strip search of the refugees. After being questioned, everyone in Fritsch's group of travelers got on to buses and were taken to a small village as planned.

One more unexpected twist awaited them, however. Some people who wore mountaineering clothing and carried equipment for rugged travel approached the group of refugees and took them aside. They explained that they were underground activists. They wanted a financial contribution, so that they could continue the process of helping Poles escape through mountain terrain to the safety of Slovakia and Hungary. The self-described activists never threatened or demanded that they be paid, but knowing they were so close to liberty made the refugees even more cautious. They gave some money to these people, who thanked everyone and slipped away.

Finally they reached the home of a pharmacist in the Slovakian village where my father had been taken. Nathan Nudel and his wife bid the group farewell, and there was a family reunion of sorts. It should have been triumphant. My father, mother, sister, Uncle Ushier, Aunt Hanka and my cousins Avram and Olga had escaped from a country that was being turned into a slaughterhouse for Jews. There should have been great joy and celebration shared at that pharmacist's home. Instead, and despite the lack of immediate threat, the mood became instantly tense. My father told the others that he had recently been in jail for three days. The Slovakian police had picked him up and accusing him of illegal entry, even though Fritsch had provided him with papers that should have avoided that problem.

Fortunately, Monek had been released, but it still seemed that they were not entirely safe. Slovakia itself was governed by a fascist regime. Under the leadership of Jozef Tiso, the country had one political party, run by the Catholic clergy, and they were closely associated with Germany. At the end of 1940, there had been almost 90,000 Jews in Slovakia, but between March and October, 1942, most had been rounded up and turned over to Germany at the border. Fortunately, when Tiso learned, in the autumn of 1942, of the slaughter going on in Poland, he refused to deport the remaining 24,000 Jews in his country. My family arrived in 1943 during a period of relative safety for Jewish refugees in Slovakia.

Nevertheless, most Jews who made it across the Polish-Slovakian border continued on to Hungary. Ushier, Hanka, and their children did not stay long at the pharmacist's house. A van had been arranged to take them to Budapest, where they had already rented an apartment, but misfortune followed them to their new life. Ten days after my mother and father had said goodbye to Ushier and

Hanka, hoping to rest a little in Slovakia, a telegram arrived at the pharmacist's home where they were staying. Hanka was in a Budapest hospital. She was in great pain and about to have gall bladder surgery. Avram was at home taking care of baby Olga so Ushier could stay in the hospital with Hanka, and he asked the rest of the family to come and help him with the children.

So Monek and Hela hurriedly made arrangements to get to Budapest, paying to secure space alongside an engineer on a Budapest-bound coal train. Ewa, sitting too close to the furnace that fed the engine, had a burning ember jump out and land on her green coat. Before they could put it out, it had burned a small hole with a brown ring around it. My parents would not be able to buy her another coat for a while, and that scorch mark would remind them all of the sudden, sad journey that brought them to Budapest. In Ushier's Budapest apartment, they found little Avram carrying his baby sister and trying to calm her cries. They immediately stepped in to take care of the children while Ushier spent time in the hospital with Hanka.

When Hanka was released from the hospital, she and Ushier were able to discuss the instability of their situation. They didn't know whether they would be pulled in off the street and questioned, as Monek had been. It was very possible that the papers they had been given to enable them to travel from Slovakia to Hungary could be challenged. They did not have the protection of the International Red Cross. The danger was far from over.

CHAPTER 8

Dr. Kotarba

Deportations of Jews and others from Slovakia, where my family had initially escaped to, required refugees to flee to the next unoccupied nation. Beginning in 1942, a huge wave of refugees — many, like my own family, from Poland — poured southwards from Slovakia into Hungary. My family arrived in the summer of 1943.

Hungary had declared war on the Soviet Union in 1941 and was aligned, in a limited way, with Germany. The governance of Hungary was complicated: though officially a kingdom, the country was in fact governed by a series of short-lived prime ministers, who served as heads of government, and by Admiral Miklós Horthy, who served as head of state in the monarch's stead and as governor-regent, with the power to convene and dissolve parliament, dismiss prime ministers, and command the army.

Caught between pressure from Germany and international outrage about Nazi terror, Admiral Horthy tried to remain as neutral as possible regarding Germany's mission to annihilate Europe's Jews, but he dared not confront Hitler. Hungarian Prime Minister Miklós Kállay had communicated with the Allies, hoping to side with them in exchange for protection against Germany and/or the Soviets. But his communiqués were intercepted by the Germans, who demanded that Hungary continue to side with them or risk invasion and occupation. Furthermore, Horthy had received information that if the Nazis invaded Hungary, massacring Jews as they had in other countries, the Allied forces would likely begin a bombing campaign in Budapest. At the same time, he had a nationalist, violent, anti-Semitic group in his own country, the *Nyilas* or Arrow Cross Party. Be that as it may, Polish gentile and Jewish refugees entered Hungary in great numbers during that period.

Many children were abandoned in the chaos of the war, sometimes out of negligence, sometimes out of desperation by parents who were trying to keep them alive. My father heard about a Polish man who owned a building in Vác, a town about twenty miles from Budapest, which was being used as an orphanage for such children. It was called the School for Children of Polish Officers and was run by a Polish priest. To the outside world, the young people living there were Christians, abandoned due to fathers who were in the military. In reality, the students were Jewish children, shielded from deportation and execution by the combined efforts of people of various nationalities and faiths.

In Budapest, my father met one of the people involved in establishing and running this orphanage: Henryk Sławik. Sławik had been one of about 100,000 Polish refugees in Hungary after the 1939 Nazi occupation. He was lucky to be alive. In a prisoner of war camp in Hungary, as a former journalist and soldier, he had met József Antall, Sr., who was responsible for civilian refugees on behalf of the Hungarian Ministry of Foreign Affairs. (Antall Senior's son, József Jr., eventually became post-communist Hungary's prime minister.) Antall Senior befriended and supported Sławik, whose fluent German got him appointed to head Hungary's Citizen's Committee for Help for Polish Refugees.

Sławik's benevolent work, funded by both Hungary and the Polish government in exile, allowed many displaced persons and prisoners of war to find work and place their children in schools. One of Sławik's many missions was to find Jews hiding in Hungary. He would then use cooperative Catholic priests to create false birth certificates attesting that the holders were Christians. He was also to appoint a commanding officer of a camp of Polish Jews, who enabled them all to escape before they could be killed. He helped provide false Polish passports designating approximately five thousand Jews as Catholics, thus saving their lives. Sławik introduced my father to many of the people who helped him in Budapest. He also arranged for Monek to obtain new papers, which established his identity as "Karoly Kotarba." My mother and sister took on the name Kotarba as well, but their first names stayed the same. This allowed them to hide their Jewish identities and to remain in Hungary.

Eventually, in the spring or summer of 1944, the Nazis arrested both Sławik and József Antall. Because of Antall's strong standing in the Hungarian government, the Nazis beat and tortured Sławik, trying to establish Antall's complicity in saving people from the Nazis. Sławik refused, instead taking all responsibility himself. His actions were especially heroic given that Hungarian friends had arranged three visas for him and his wife and daughter, which would have enabled the family to flee to the safety of Switzerland at any time.

Sławik's refusal to implicate Antall saved Antall's life. Sławik himself was sent to the Gusen concentration-camp complex near Mathausen with some of his fellow Polish activists. In August, 1944, he was hanged. His wife, Jadwiga, survived the brutality of the Ravensbruck concentration camp, the largest death camp for women in the German Reich. Fifty miles north of Berlin, Ravensbruck held up to 50,000 inmates. In addition to horrific living conditions, the female interns at Ravensbruck, mostly Poles, were subjected to medical experiments. Yet Jadwiga persevered. After the war, she found their daughter, who had been living under the protection of the Antall family in Hungary.ok

Overall, Sławik helped save over 30,000 Polish refugees. Today he is known as "the Polish Wallenberg," a reference to Swedish diplomat Raoul Wallenberg, who saved the lives of thousands of Budapest Jews during the war by making them honorary citizens of Sweden, providing them with documents that prevented Nazis from rounding them up for extermination.

My father saw the orphanage as an opportunity to begin fulfilling the vow he had made as a prisoner in Janowska. The war was clearly far from over. For now, however, he had escaped the camp and reunited with his family, and here were children who needed help. He became involved in managing the School for Children of Polish Officers, as did another fellow Pole, Wladislaw Bratkowski, and his wife, Mina.

Like my father, Bratkowski had false papers. His real name was Brettler. He had been an attorney in Poland when the Soviet Union invaded from the east. Living in a town called Kozowa, where two thousand Jews were eventually killed, Brettler had organized a *Judenrat* and helped facilitate the escape of his fellow Jews. His wife and mother were arrested, but a Jew who collaborated with the Germans effected their release. Brettler and his wife avoided the total liquidation of Jews in Kozowa and Kolomyja by obtaining false papers and entering Hungary, arriving in Budapest in April, 1943. By working with cooperative Hungarian Jews, he continued helping his fellow Polish Jews enter the new country.

Through the orphanage at Vác, the orphanage administrator, Franciszek Swider — thanks to the efforts of Antall and Sławik, and with the help of Brettler and my father — provided safe haven for almost a hundred boys and girls, from ages 3 to 19. All the children and staff were given forged documents, attesting to their supposed gentile background. The orphanage was sanctioned by the Hungarian government, which felt a responsibility to take care of the young refugees, yet most of the children only spoke Polish, so they could not be sent to Hungarian doctors or schools. The government also welcomed Poland's taking some of the financial responsibility for the care of homeless Polish children in their country.

In July 1943, Brettler and his wife were both arrested — not because of the orphanage in Vác but in connection with their identity papers. They were sent to a labor camp on the Polish-Hungarian border but later released, and Brettler and my father continued to collaborate on the general organization of the school and the structuring of its classes. These courses secretly included the history of Judaism and Zionism, to make sure that, even though the children pretended to be Christian, they would be aware of their own heritage. The orphanage even managed to celebrate Passover, adhering to the tradition of avoiding leavened bread by eating potatoes all week. My father was also the doctor at the orphanage, attending not only to their bodily needs but offering psychological counseling as well; many of the children had endured terrifying circumstances before coming to Vác and bore those psychological scars.

The School for the Children of Polish Officers's need to maintain the front that it was filled with gentile, not Jewish, children was done with the assistance of another hero of the resistance during the war: Monsignor Angelo Rotta, papal nuncio for Pope Pius XII. Rotta was instrumental in setting up an international ghetto in Budapest, in which 25,000 Jews were housed in modern apartment buildings and protected by the governments of Sweden, Switzerland, Portugal and Spain. It was Rotta who got permission from the Vatican to issue protective passes stating that the holders were Christian. These passes were issued to anyone, primarily Jews, by priests who agreed to issue the passes without a demand for authentication. Approximately 15,000 of these Vatican-approved passes were issued prior to the Nazi invasion of Hungary.

Pope Pius XII has been historically criticized for not being more vocal in his criticism of the Nazis in his encyclicals, but his defenders remind critics that the Vatican had to contend with Benito Mussolini in its own country and, later, the German occupation of Italy. The Pope's use of Rotta in Hungary was one of a number of examples of Vatican efforts to provide aid to European Jews. In 2012, Yad Vashem changed an inscription to say that the Vatican under Pope Pius XII was party to a "considerable number of secret rescue activities."

Another gentile who risked his life in connection with the orphanage at Vác was Dr. Pavel Suharczik, a priest who cooperated with Sławik, my father, and others to conduct Catholic services at the orphanage, supporting the impression that the children were Polish Christians. The children all attended services each Sunday at a local church, and with both Suharczik and Angelo Rotta visiting at Vác, the authorities did not question the religious background of the children. The school was officially designated as a part of the Polish government in exile in September of 1943.

I heard about the orphanage firsthand from Edward Herman, one of the first children brought to the school, whom I found in 2015 — then age 83 — living in St. Petersburg, Florida. I had seen a documentary, *Never Forget to Lie*, on the PBS series *Frontline*, which detailed Herman's life in Vác, living with my father and others. I searched for his address and found it on the internet. I immediately wrote to him and left a voice mail message. Six days later he called, and we became friends.

Herman told me that his mother, who was blonde and Aryan looking, feared that he would be taken from her in Poland. She therefore obtained false identity papers for herself, her daughter, and Herman, and sent him to Hungary to live with a family friend. The friend, however, abandoned him, leaving Herman, at the age of 11, living on the streets of Budapest, alone, hungry, terrified, not speaking the language. "I knew that if apprehended by the police," he said, "I could be deported back to Poland, a certain death sentence." A kind woman, Ms. Schweitzer, who saw him on the street in Budapest crying, took him to Vác, to the Polish orphanage.

In the beginning days of the school in Vác, Herman recalled, the building lacked enough furnishings for all the children who had found refuge there. "Initially, we did not have enough beds," he told me. "I had to share my bed with a younger boy, whose parents had been murdered by the Nazis. He experienced nightmares every night and as a result, would wet our communal bed."

Ed Herman saved a 1943 photograph of all the children at Vác, which included my sister Ewa. He sent me a copy so that I could see, for the first time, my father as Dr. Kotarba at the School for Children of Polish Officers, along with Franciszek Swider and Mina Bratkowski sitting in the same row.

As a Holocaust survivor, Ed would give presentations in schools to share his experiences during the war. After he and I established contact, he approached a Tampa newspaper to relate the discovery. "I remember his father clearly," Ed Herman told the reporter. "At one point, while I was living at the orphanage, I was very sick with high fevers and was treated by Dr. Osterweil's father." Reading his quote in that newspaper article moved me deeply. "I was born on Hanukkah, the holiday of miracles," Ed said. "This new link to my past is another small miracle in my life."

The orphanage in Vác that my father became involved with was one of several efforts being taken on behalf of abandoned and orphaned Jewish children in Hungary. Organizations such as the Welfare Bureau for Hungarian Jews (MIPI) and the National Hungarian Jewish Assistance Campaign (OMZSA) were already providing funds for refugees in Hungary in 1942. Through the influence of Sławik, the OMZSA had contributed money for the orphanage in Vác. These organizations and other lesser-known ones were also funding houses for Jewish children in Budapest. These were noble and righteous programs, but such solutions assumed an eventual diplomatic solution to the German threats to Hungary. Unfortunately, no such diplomatic solution emerged. The Nazi invasion of Hungary in March of 1944 would threaten all Jews in the country, including children without families, whether they were clearly identified as Jews or even, as in the orphanage in Vác, living with identification papers that made them appear to be gentile.

CHAPTER 9

In Nazi-controlled Hungary

When the Nazis finally tired of Hungarian attempts at diplomacy, they invaded, on March 19, 1944. Three days after the Nazis entered the country, a new government was established, with Prime Minister Döme Sztójay, unlike Admiral Horthy, cooperating fully with Berlin. Labor unions were immediately dissolved, and political leaders were jailed. Jews were forced to wear the yellow Star of David, and deportations in massive numbers to Auschwitz began. It would turn out to be the most rapid and lethal period of annihilation of any group of Jews during the entire Holocaust. Between May 14 and July 18, over 430,000 Hungarian Jews were forced onto 48 trains to Auschwitz, where most of them were immediately executed in gas chambers.

While walking down the street in Vác one day, my father was stopped by police doing random inspections of papers. He was accused of possessing forged documents and brought into a police station for interrogation. It was unclear whether the police knew that the documents identifying him as Dr. Kotarba really were forged, but what saved Monek was a different document, a card that identified him as a physician of the International Committee of the Red Cross (IRC) in Hungary.

Monek had this card because of a man named Ottó Komoly. In the late summer of 1944, Komoly, who was head of the Hungarian Zionist Association, was asked to head the International Committee of the Red Cross in Hungary's Section A, charged with the rescue of children. Komoly was Monek's main contact at the Budapest Aid and Rescue Committee, an organization founded to aid Jews fleeing to the presumed relative safety of Hungary, which Komoly headed.

As an officer during the First World War, Komoly had been wounded on the Italian front and decorated for his bravery. Because of his celebrity within the country, the Nazis did not persecute him. Respect for him was so great among Hungarians that even the anti-Semitic nationalist Hungarian group the Arrow Cross (*Nyilas*), whose militias often killed Jews at will, dared not arrest him.

Komoly was a man of exceptional bravery and decency. He had the opportunity to leave the dangers of his home country with his family for Palestine in 1939, but he refused to take advantage of his unique position. He also used the Relief and Rescue Committee to try to resist Eichmann's policies for Jews and non-Jews alike, utilizing his connections with clergy, such as Father Suharczik, and politicians, such as the son of Admiral Horthy.

Perhaps his connection with Komoly gave my father confidence, or perhaps his reaction was merely a result of his innate stubbornness, but when his interrogators ordered him to strip so they could see whether he was circumcised, he flatly refused. He reminded them that they were in defiance of IRC orders simply by bringing him in for questioning. He insisted that he had immunity under terms of the IRC and promised to inform the IRC if he was not allowed to leave. After hours of repetitive questioning, my father was allowed to walk out of the police station and return to his apartment and his orphanage, but he had to make a compromise. The Hungarian police suspected that some Jews were hidden in the "Polish orphanage," and Monek had to promise that the orphanage would close within two weeks and all its inhabitants would "disappear."

My father would not actually close the orphanage, however. He would keep his promise to close down the operation in Vác, but he started making arrangements to move the children from Vác to Budapest, where he had more contacts and felt he would be better able to protect the children. With the help of organizations such as the Aid and Rescue Committee, Monek was able to find room in several apartment buildings to house the children. Once this was arranged, my father went back to Wladislaw Brettler, who had been so important in setting up the Vác location. Together, they organized train trips to Budapest with fifteen to twenty children at a time. Finally, around 80 of the protected children, Jewish and gentile, were relocated in Budapest.

Another of Monek's contacts in Budapest, Rezső (Rudolf) Kasztner, had been Komoly's partner in founding the Budapest Aid and Rescue Committee. My uncle Ushier learned about Kasztner's activities through my father, and one day he took young Avram to Kasztner's office to offer him money to let the boy be one of those to escape the Hungarian deportations. Avram, years later, remembered sitting outside the office, hearing his father speaking in German, pleading with Kasztner on his behalf.

Shortly after the Kasztner meeting, Ushier and Hanka sat down with Avram in their small apartment for a somber discussion. They explained the hopes they had of immigrating to Palestine one day to live together in peace, but they made clear to him the increasing dangers of life in Budapest. "I know it's not what any of us want," Ushier explained, "but we can get you on a train — without us — to go to Palestine and live with friends until the war is over. It's the best we can do, and it has to be done quickly. Will you agree to go?" Avram, even at his young age, understood the implications of staying in Budapest. He told me years later, "it took me no time to say yes."

A few days later, on June 30, 1944, Ushier and Hanka took Avram to the train station in Budapest. They had given him forty American dollars, which they hid in the heel of one of his shoes. Hanka had baked him his favorite poppy-seed cake, cut into pieces so that he could eat it on the way. They introduced him to a man named Yossi, who would pose as Avram's father, along with a woman who pretended to be his mother. Yossi lived on a *kibbutz* in Palestine, and Kasztner regularly used him to help Jews in Hungary sneak out of the country. Avram said a quick, emotional farewell to Ushier and Hanka and boarded the train with his new makeshift family. Yossi reassured the boy as they got on board, but whatever security Avram might have felt was quickly crushed.

The train was inhumanely crowded. People sat on the floor and were unable to stretch their arms or legs without hitting the passengers around them. The adults and children who sat near Avram spoke little and avoided eye contact. Knowing that deportees to the death camps had been told that they were merely going to temporary labor camps, many passengers must have wondered if Kasztner's train was really a ride to freedom or a cruel hoax that would drive them to their deaths. But it was a chance many were willing to take — many more than could fit comfortably into those jammed, stifling compartments.

The only ease the passengers found was in taking off their shoes, but Avram could not even do this, for fear that the money he had been given for survival would be lost or taken. When the train crossed the border into Romania and the compartments were checked, some of refugees around Avram teased him and told him to take off his shoes. He ignored them. When the train arrived in Bucharest, Avram whispered goodbye to Yossi, as it was there that he was to transfer to another train.

Avram stepped down from the train, stretching his arms and legs, which were painfully cramped. He saw a bench nearby and sat down. Without even realizing it, his eyelids lowered and he fell asleep.

He awakened to a strong male hand shaking him. He opened his eyes to see a Romanian soldier. Avram couldn't understand what the soldier said, but he saw where he was pointing. The train Avram was supposed to catch was pulling out of the station.

Avram leaped to his feet off the bench and ran with all the speed he could muster. The train was gaining momentum. Avram approached one of the cars and grabbed onto the door handle, hoisting himself up and into the compartment. His next stop was Sofia, Bulgaria, where he spent a full day and night before boarding yet another train, this one destined for Istanbul, Turkey. There, he had to wait a few days before a fishing boat could take him across the Black Sea. In Istanbul, a world apart from anything Avram had ever seen, he remembered seeing scores of Turkish soldiers, their heads shaven to prevent the spread of lice. Turkish officers, he noted, got to keep their hair long. Avram passed some of the time watching a film. The movie was in Turkish, so Avram couldn't understand the dialogue, but the film appeared to be about the British Army soundly defeating the Germans in the war. At that point, sadly, it was only a movie.

The fishing boat took Avram to Damascus, Syria, where he then traveled to Haifa. There, a bus with black curtains took eleven children, all illegal immigrants, to a pension on Mount Carmel, originally run by Henrietta Szold, the Zionist leader and founder of Hadassah, and administered by the Jewish Agency in Palestine.

Avram's extraordinary trip was still not over. In addition to the forty dollars hidden in his shoe, he had been given two letters. The manager of the pension called the two people the letters were addressed to, to notify them of Avram's arrival: Yeshayahu Spiro, who became a radio broadcasting executive at Kol Israel, the nascent state's official radio station, had known Ushier and Hanka in Tarnów. Jacov "Kuba" Fleischer, another family friend, arranged to take Avram to Merhavia, the *kibbutz* where he would live.

Not long after Avram escaped to safety, his father was stopped and questioned on the street in Budapest, just as my father had been in Vác. Ushier may have been reported by a Hungarian neighbor, who suspected Ushier of being in the country illegally. The authorities saw that he had come into the country from Slovakia. In the hysteria of the time, that was sufficient reason to deport him to the Mauthausen-Gusen concentration camp in Austria, twelve miles east of Linz, the birthplace of Adolf Hitler.

Mauthausen grew so rapidly after 1940 that it became one of the largest labor camps run by the Nazis in all of Europe. Subcamps included munitions factories, quarries, mines, arms factories, and even an assembly plant for fighter planes. The camp was intended for the intelligentsia, those of upper, educated classes, who were expected to work until they died in service of the Reich. In fact, the Reich Main Security Office had a particular German nickname for Mauthausen: *Knochenmühle* — the bone crusher.

My uncle's spirit, though, could not be crushed, even at that camp. There is one brief story about his time there that has stuck in my mind. One day an SS officer was looking over some prisoners, not all of them Jews, and noticed Ushier's last name. "Osterweil," the officer said with a smirk. "Isn't that a Jewish name?"

Ushier saw the Nazi soldier's last name was Miller. "Miller," he said with an edge to his voice. "Isn't that a Jewish name?" It was a terrible risk, but Ushier was a shrewd man. His comment was enough to persuade the German to leave him alone.

While Monek was transferring the orphanage to Budapest, Hela and Ewa were still in Vác. They lived in a rented room in the house of a Jewish family, one of only two remaining in the town, the others having been deported. They lived next to a shared courtyard. Monek and Hela could only afford to pay for the bedroom but not the adjacent kitchen. The Jewish family opened a hole in the wall to allow placing a pot on the furnace. In addition, Hela had a field furnace that used alcohol capsules for fuel to boil water. The landlord's wife, who was a good cook, taught Hela how to prepare various Jewish dishes such as gefilte fish with nuts. (Vác was in a semirural area, which gave the inhabitants better access to surrounding orchards than was available in larger cities.)

When it snowed outside, Hela used to go out and rub herself with snow as a way of washing and refreshing herself. Ewa remembers watching her with fascination, wondering how she could tolerate the cold. For her part, Ewa refused to go to sleep unless Hela first lay on her bed to warm it up for her. On the coldest nights, Hela would warm up a brick on the furnace and then use it to warm up the bed.

Until the Germans invaded Hungary and entered Budapest in March, 1944, my mother and sister stayed in Vác, with my father shuttling back and forth between Vác and Budapest, where the rest of the children were placed in safe houses or apartments. (When Monek brought Hela and Ewa to Budapest after the Russians took the city near the end of the War, my sister remembers my father showing them a building where some of the children had been living. A bomb had blown off the face of the building, exposing the apartments' kitchens, bedrooms, and other living quarters.)

On his trips back and forth from Budapest, Monek would bring back gifts to Ewa, to keep her spirits up. Once, he purchased a book in German, Hans Christian Andersen's *Most Beautiful Fairy Tales* (*Schönste Märchen*). He read the German and translated it into Polish for her, so she could understand. Another time, he carried in a small suitcase. When opened, it had a doll in the left section, along with a makeshift little closet to hold the clothing for the doll. Ewa was delighted.

For Hela's birthday, December 21, 1944, Monek decided to surprise her. He found a decorative ashtray in the market and wrapped it in paper. The night before her birthday, he gave Ewa the present and a flashlight so she could secretly sneak in and hang it above Hela's bed, to surprise her in the morning. Ewa enjoyed the feeling of being a co-conspirator with her father; in fact, as Ewa told me years later, Hela was only pretending to be asleep. She wanted Ewa to be able to enjoy this small moment of fun.

With the help of another Polish refugee, Hela and Mina Brettler obtained work permits as cherry pickers. They spent only one day actually picking cherries, but the permits gave them a something to show police if they were stopped, to prove they had a reason to be in town. Hela also took Ewa to regular church services, to keep up the appearance that they were good Catholics.

Hela was very particular about her appearance, always meticulous about how she dressed and kept her hair. Even in those tumultuous days, she used to go to a hairdresser who worked out of her backyard. She would heat the water to wash her clients' hair on an open fireplace in the yard. Ewa, who liked to run around while

Hela got her hair done, once stumbled on one of the hot stones and burned her foot so badly that she could not walk on it.

This was particularly problematic because there was an air raid soon afterward. The building Hela and Ewa lived in, like many in the town, was not safe to stay in while bombs were falling. During the frequent air raids, people would run to the catacombs of a church with rough-hewn stone walls. This time, Hela had to carry Ewa to the church. By the time they got underground, the space was very crowded, and Ewa needed room to lie down. The only place Hela could find was where an old door had been blown off its hinges and lay on the cold stone floor.

Hela lay Ewa down carefully on the door, but soon my sister began shivering. My mother realized they would be in the shelter for a long time, and she felt she needed to go back to the apartment and get a blanket for Ewa. It was not safe to go back, but my mother always followed her instincts.

Hela asked people nearby to watch Ewa, and to their astonishment she pushed her way through the throng of frightened people and forced her way up the stairs and outside with the bombers dropping their payloads on the edge of town. She rushed home to get the blanket, but on the way back, explosions rocked the ground, barring her path. Buildings were splintered and huge pieces of pavement were blasted skyward. Hela tried to continue, but the intensity of the explosions grew so strong that she understood she would likely never make it back to the church, so she found a nearby alcove and curled into a ball, head down, waiting out the continuous pounding of bombs. Then she returned to the catacombs with the blanket. She wrapped it around Ewa and carried her back to their apartment.

When Monek was in Vác, he repeatedly warned the two Jewish families remaining there that they were too exposed, too noticeable.

Monek suggested that they move to Budapest, where it would be easier to hide in the big city. He managed to convince an older daughter of one family, who lived in Budapest, to stay away from Vác. He often told her family in Vác to hide, but they would not listen. As the Germans entered the town, the remaining Jews were discovered and taken away. The older daughter survived.

In Budapest, the original group from the orphanage was constantly growing, as more and more children in need of help appeared. While my father provided medical services, classes, and general management of the orphanage, he knew he could not possibly handle the expanding numbers on his own. He urged the children already in their teens to take on responsibility for guiding and reassuring the younger ones. It was a wise decision. The separation from their families, compounded by the daily threat of death, was incredibly difficult, and most of the children had suffered severe trauma. The support of an older child — who had been through similar experiences themselves — was in some ways more helpful than that of an adult.

There were, of course, many adults who helped with the orphanage. Ottó Komoly continued to provide invaluable assistance, using his connections, especially József Antall at the Ministry of Foreign Affairs, to provide resources, including food, for the children. Pavel Suharczik, the priest who had conducted the Christian prayer services in Vác to help hide the fact that the children were Jewish, provided a similar service in Budapest. He convinced the police that he was conducting religious services, when in fact he was teaching the children Hungarian. Wladislaw Brettler joined my father in giving the children lessons in Jewish history and religious thought, so they would not lose a sense of their true heritage.

My aunt Hanka was instrumental in feeding the children, and she did not appreciate Monek's interference in matters of the kitchen. Monek asked Hanka to make beans, which required more wood for longer boiling than other food. Hanka resisted, wanting to give the kids more variety. Monek convinced her to make beans daily and leave the pasta for later, when they ran out of wood. They could use paper or other materials to make the fire to cook pasta, he said, as it required less heat to cook.

Such considerations seemed less important after July 2, 1944, as the American and British air forces began dropping mines in the Danube and bombing the city of Budapest. They also dropped leaflets condemning Hitler for the murder of Jews in Auschwitz and promising retribution if the deportations continued. Hitler, wary of a general uprising in the midst of this bombing campaign, and with the Wehrmacht retreating before Russian forces along the entire eastern front, stopped the deportations on July 8.

When the Soviet army crossed Hungary's border in September, Horthy announced he was going to sign an armistice with the Soviet Union. Despite the inevitability of their defeat, the Nazis would not relinquish Hungary, which provided much of the oil for their war effort. Horthy was kidnapped by SS officers and forced to abdicate his role as Regent. Instead, Hitler installed Ferenc Szálasi, head of the Arrow Cross, as prime minister and head of state. For the local population, in addition to the dangers from the Nazis, the Arrow Cross Party, starvation, and illness, there was the new challenge of the combined Allied-Russian bombing campaign, which began in earnest after Horthy was deposed.

Throughout Hungary, the Germans began to retreat, destroying railway, road, and communication systems as they went and creating even more misery. People now had no direct way to check on the whereabouts and safety of relatives and friends. But Ferenc

Szálasi's rule lasted less than six months. On his first day in office, the Red Army had already penetrated deep into Hungary. There was no way, in the chaos of the bombing campaign and German retreat, to organize a military defense of Hungary. By November of 1944, two-thirds of the country was under Russian control.

There was hope in the Hungarian countryside that the partial occupation of the country by the Russians would bring some peace and stability. In some ways life was indeed safer. But my mother, whose blonde hair had helped convince onlookers that she was not Jewish, found that her appearance worked against her with the Russian soldiers who patrolled Vác.

One day, she was on her way into town to fix the family's small camp furnace when four Russian soldiers in a Jeep accosted her on the street. Hela was able to communicate with them in basic Russian but was very anxious. One soldier accused her, partly teasing, "You're German. You're a spy." She denied it, frozen with fear. They took her for questioning to their military police station. "I like her," suggested that particular soldier, and continued to question her. Hela insisted she was not German, and the soldier convinced his peers to let her go. The same soldier came several times to where they lived, trying to make contact with Hela. One time he handed a coin to Ewa over the fence. Hela pinched her, signaling not to take it, out of fear that later they could be accused of stealing from a Russian soldier.

Many other women in Hungary had much worse experiences. Estimates of the number of girls and women raped in Budapest by Russian soldiers range from 5,000 to 200,000. No one will ever know the exact figure.

To avoid the attentions of that soldier, and for greater security in general, Hela and Ewa found another apartment building to live in.

It had a front gate which provided some additional protection. They tried to minimize the time they were outside on the streets of Vác, with no idea how my father and other family members were faring in Budapest. It was not until February 1945 that my mother and my sister were able to join my father there, moving with him and some of the rescued children into a small house on Kövér Lajos Street.

By November 8, 1944, the Russians had a temporary stronghold on the outskirts of Pest, but the Nazis, refusing to give up the capital, dug in, and the horrible siege of Budapest, which lasted seven bloody, terrifying weeks, began. At stake inside the city was the fate of about 70,000 German and Hungarian soldiers and 800,000 civilians. A Jewish ghetto had been established, and even though deportations had stopped, the dragging of men, women, and children to the Danube to be drowned now became a common occurrence. The Arrow Cross, sensing the beginning of the end for them and the Nazis, increased the speed and intensity of their persecution. They made many attempts to take even children who were under the protection of the IRC and transfer them to the ghetto, where their slaughter would be eventually accomplished.

The lives of some of these Jewish children in Budapest were preserved from Arrow Cross raids in ingenious ways. Many shelters, like the orphanages, identified themselves as Christian institutions. The manager of one site told an Arrow Cross officer that all the children inside were relatives of Hungarian soldiers bravely fighting at the Russian front, which stymied any further attempts. Another house used the excuse that the children were in fact Hungarian refugees, who had fled the advance of the Russians for whatever safety could be garnered in Budapest.

On Christmas Eve, 1944, Jewish children in protected houses were outside singing Christmas carols, to help convince the Arrow

Cross that, as good Christians, they should not be molested in any way. Other Budapest homes housing Jewish refugees announced that the house was quarantined due to serious illnesses. One house went so far as to hang the Arrow Cross flag out front, which had been left there days before by an angry militia man with murderous intent. The IRC moved some Jewish children — healthy as well as sick — into hospitals, where their safety was more likely to be guaranteed. More than once, a Zionist Youth member got hold of a Nazi or Arrow Cross uniform and brought Jewish children to the protection of an official building.

My mother told me later of one heroic young Jewish man, among many. Rafi Ben-Shalom, member of the Halutz ("Pioneer") underground movement in Hungary, would don a stolen Arrow Cross uniform and enter the ghetto on the pretense of taking children away for execution. When Ben-Shalom and his peers had taken the children safely across the bridge and away from the ghetto, he would remove the uniform, explain that he was rescuing them, and bring the children to one of the safe houses set up in Budapest. The children who went through this experience later described feeling terrified, to the point of peeing in their pants — only to find, to their immense relief, that they were being rescued.

On Christmas Day, 1944, the Russians entered Buda from the west, advancing through quiet, picturesque Castle Hill and across bridges into Pest, where battle fronts were drawn up. The next day, they cut a road connecting Budapest to Vienna, completing the encirclement of the city. What would follow in Pest was often hand-to-hand and house-to-house fighting, in one neighborhood after another.

This period, when the city was under siege with aerial bombardment, street fighting and Russian artillery, was the most horrifying time for street children. One of those children, whom I met many years later, was named Shlomo Arad, originally Salomon Goldberg. He and his brother, Wolf (Ze'ev), had lived with their parents in Austria but were then deported back to country of origin, Poland. The boys' father was sent to a labor camp and never heard from again. Their mother trained them in Catholic prayers, so they would not be persecuted as Jews, and arranged for false papers identifying them as Staszek and Juzek Robutka.

Attempting to enter Hungary near the border of Slovakia, close to the town of Košice, the two boys and their mother were caught by border guards, who, Shlomo recalled, wore hats with feathers. They were jailed near the end of 1942. By the time Zionist operatives negotiated the release of the boys, their mother was no longer in jail, and no one could account for her whereabouts.

Living by themselves and by their wits on the streets of the capital, the Arad brothers used the air raids to their benefit. When Budapest residents dashed from their homes for air raid shelters, sometimes four or five times in a day, Shlomo would secure his brother in a safe place such as the basement of a building. After waiting for the occupants to hurry out, Shlomo would run into their hastily abandoned apartments and take whatever food he found. Sometimes, the meal was still on the table, warm, left in dishes by fleeing families. When the air raid siren sounded the all-clear signal to that neighborhood, Shlomo quickly left the apartment before its residents returned.

Shlomo and his brother knew they could not survive that way for long. They recalled that their mother had told them about a monastery that might be a safe place to hide. They found the monastery, which housed developmentally disabled children, and stayed there for a while. One day, returning after a day of foraging for food, they returned to find the children were gone. The Arrow Cross had taken them all and dumped them in the Danube.

By the end of December, 1944, the boys were living in the Jewish orphanage at 25–27 Queen Vilma Road in Budapest. During this period these houses were under the protection of the International Red Cross, which provided cover but could not guarantee safety. One day, the Arrow Cross militia entered the building and demanded that the children come out and stand in twos, then march down to the Danube, which seemed like "a long walk on a very cold night," as Shlomo remembered later. The occupation by the Nazis and their sympathizers was in its death throes, but the Arrow Cross were not deterred. Like other systematic raids, the end result of this half-mile march would be machine-gun fire and a watery grave. Some children and their adult caregivers were indeed shot, their bodies blasted into the water of the Danube. Fortunately for Shlomo and Ze'ev, they did not reach the river. An air-raid siren sounded, and the boys fell to the ground along with everyone else. Shortly afterward bombs began falling in the city. In the confusion of the moment, Shlomo and his brother ran from the group and escaped without being shot by the militia. "People were shouting 'Üvegház!' to indicate the direction of the escape," Shlomo remembered. "This was the Glass House, which was under the auspices of the Swiss Embassy in Budapest."[6] The two brothers stayed there until the end of the war.

---

6   The Glass House (once a glass factory) at 29 Vadász Street in Budapest housed thousands of Jews, including members of the Jewish youth underground, thanks to the efforts of Carl Lutz, the Swiss vice-consul in Budapest. Today the building is a museum. Lutz is believed to have saved 62,000 Jews from the Holocaust. (See for example Marian Holmes, "Fife Rescuers of Those Threatened by the Holocaust," *Smithsonian*, February 24, 2009.)

My father eventually found the Goldberg brothers under an overpass. He brought them back to one of the orphanages, where they became almost like part of the family. They also grew close to another family, Mrs. Malinowska and her three daughters, Matilda, Stefa, and Gusta. Shlomo became well known in the orphanage by the affectionate nickname "the Hungarian kid."

Shlomo Arad ended up in Israel, where he became a noted photographer and photo curator. When our mother died, in August of 2009, he came to offer condolences to Ewa. My sister introduced us, and he told me his story. Monek, Shlomo told us, saved him and his brother's lives. Shlomo had visited my father to thank him, when my father was the medical director in Be'er Ya'akov and Shlomo has just graduated from the Israeli Defense Force's officers' school at the IDF. This moved me even further — how great he must have made my dad feel, what a mensch Shlomo was.

In Budapest, the fighting and confusion continued for weeks. On February 11, 1945, after six weeks of heavy fighting and simultaneous attacks on entrenched German troops from three sides, the Russians took Gellért Hill in Buda. From this location, which overlooked the rest of the city, the Russian artillery spotters could call down a merciless shelling of remaining Nazi strongholds, now wedged into a two-kilometer area and stricken with disease and lack of food.

Two days later, the remaining German soldiers and Hungarian militia surrendered. In liberating Budapest, the Soviets had lost between 100,000 and 160,000 men. Budapest was utterly devastated. Eighty percent of the city lay in ruins, including historic sites like the Hungarian Parliament building and the Castle. All seven bridges that spanned the Danube were destroyed. Four previous prime ministers, including Ferenc Szálasi, were shot or hanged by the new Communist government. The destruction was extreme, but the Germans had finally been defeated.

Once the Nazis were gone and the Soviets were in charge, Monek was able to secure three buildings in Budapest to house the children, and they could be moved from the apartments in the center of the city. Two of the buildings were in a hilly suburban area, separated from each other only by rambling, open fields. Ottó Komoly helped him obtain plaques identifying the three buildings as orphanages protected by the IRC, a designation that meant more after the Nazis were gone. Monek's previous interactions with the Russians had helped him understand how they operated, and he became skilled at leveraging that knowledge for the benefit of the children, obtaining medications and other hard-to-find resources.

While many died, there were also many children who, like Shlomo Arad, managed to survive the transition from the German occupation to the Russian occupation in Budapest, partly through their own ingenuity and partly through luck, often with the help of people like my father. In 2008 I met a man who had been one of these children. He had contacted Zvi Osterweil, my nephew, Jerzyk's son, saying his name was George Axelrod and he wondered if Zvi was related to Monek Osterweil. George lived in New York, and I was going there to lecture at Mount Sinai Hospital as a visiting professor, so Jerzyk and I arranged a meeting with him.

George was born in Czechoslovakia to Polish parents and was a teenager when the Nazis invaded. The family lived in the border area, the Sudetenland, where many ethnic Germans lived. Both his parents were known for their nationalistic, pro-Czech opinions; following Germany's annexation of Bohemia and Moravia, they were sent to a labor camp. His mother was sent to a different camp. George and his father escaped together and made their way across the Hungarian border on foot. On the outskirts of Budapest, they found a monastery, and a cadet priest hid them there, despite the differences in their language and religious beliefs.

At a certain point this presumably safe haven became too risky, with frequent visits by the Arrow Cross militias searching for Jewish children in hiding. George and his father tried their luck in the big city of Budapest. One day George was in town and came across some German soldiers. The Germans were preparing to retreat from the advancing Soviet forces. "I was shot in the eye and the leg," Axelrod told me. "The Germans who were shooting anyone in sight. I was left under a pile of corpses." When we met face to face, I could indeed see that one of his eyes was not like the other. Then, with more emotion than I expected from someone I had just met, he told me that my father had saved his life.

He had been found by a group of IRC representatives, including my father, who were looking for survivors. They put him on a sled and took him to a safe house on Horenski Street, in the ghetto on the Buda side of the Danube. His troubles, however, were not over. While he was still recuperating from his wounds, two Russian soldiers entered the house where he was staying, looking for German deserters, who were shedding their uniforms and trying to blend in with the civilian population in Budapest. They thought George — a teenager who looked older than the rest of the children there, with fair hair and blue eyes — was German, and they pulled out their pistols to shoot him. He shouted out in Russian, "I am Jewish! Do not shoot!"

One of the soldiers put his revolver back into the holster and motioned to the other to do the same. He chuckled. "I guess the Germans did not have enough bullets for this one."

Figure 15: Franz Fritsch

Vac pictures, 1943

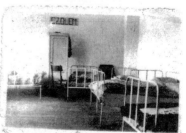

Figure 16: The School for Children of Polish Officers —
the orphanage in Vác

Figure 17: Dr. Karoly Kotarba (aka Osterweil) International Red Cross Card

Figure 18: The School for Children of Polish Officers in Vác. Five adults in center of second row, from left: Dr. Brettler and Mina; Sucharczik, the priest; unknown, Dr. Kotarba. Ewa is seated in the first row, second from left.

*Figure 20: Identification card from Avram Osterweil's
arrival in Israel*

Part Three: After the War and Looking Back

CHAPTER 10

Survival and Loss

When my family made their original escape from Poland, my aunt Hanka brought some of her heirloom jewels with her, but she hid the rest in Tarnów. When the Nazis were driven from Hungary, Hanka decided it was time to go back and recover the valuables she had hidden, despite the difficulties involved in traveling there. Hanka's first stop was Warsaw, where my family had heard that my cousin Jerzyk might be in an orphanage. She did find him there, but she was not allowed to take him with her or even to see him, because he was in quarantine due to an outbreak of diphtheria. Hanka sent word back to Hela that he was there, then moved on to Tarnów.

In Tarnów, Hanka spent time at a local community center, where she met a sixteen-year-old girl named Marisia Offen. They quickly became close. Marisia's story was typical of so many who survived the war, a combination of luck and instinct. She had been in several camps, Marisia said. The first was the Płaszów concentration camp, on the outskirts of Krakow, where her brother Aron was incarcerated and watched over her while she was helping in the kitchen. From there she was sent to the Skarżysko-Kamienna labor camp, then finally to Buchenwald, from where she was liberated.

Marisia and about twenty other survivors headed west together. Upon crossing the River Elba, they ran into a Russian patrol and were commanded to stop. The officer leading the soldiers ordered the group of refugees to follow them, and they had no choice but to do so or risk being shot. As the group trudged through the snow together, Marisia had no idea where they were being taken. Her fear spiked as a bombardment of artillery shells suddenly pounded the countryside near them. The refugees scattered, seeking protection.

The officer in charge called out to Marisia, "Come with me!" and urged her to climb onto the horse and ride behind him. Marisia did so, but, as they rode east, she had a sudden, unexplained feeling. She screamed, "I have to get off this horse!"

At first, the officer protested, but Marisia continued shrieking, and he brought the horse to a momentary halt, allowing her to slide to the ground. Just then, a shell exploded ahead of them, throwing the officer to the ground and killing the horse instantly. The officer, his face white from shock, turned to Marisia and told her that she had saved his life, and that he would take her anywhere she wanted to go. He took her to his base camp, where she was able to eat and clean up. Then he brought her to the nearest train station and bought her a ticket to Tarnów.

When Marisia arrived in Tarnów, she went to the apartment of a family friend, a Pole who still possessed some of her family's personal effects and worked for the city. Seeing Marisia in her ragged clothing, he greeted her with a bewildered look. "O my God, Marisia," he said, "I cannot believe it, you survived!" Many people he knew had disappeared, including his own parents. He provided her with clothes and a place to recover. Years later, Marisia shared with me how guilty she felt that day for having survived while the rest of her family did not. She was not yet aware that her brother Aron had also survived. The next day, her friend took her to the Jewish community center, where she might find other people who had similar experiences, and there she met Hanka.

After hearing Marisia's story, Hanka urged her, "Come to Budapest with me." She told the girl what the family had been through and how Monek and his friends and colleagues were providing for so many children. Marisia, of course, had nowhere else to go. Moved by Hanka's offer, she agreed to go to Budapest. Hanka sent a telegram telling Monek and Hela that she was bringing Marisia with her.

Hanka and Marisia traveled a long portion of the journey back to Hungary in the back of a truck filled with tomatoes. Marisia did not like tomatoes, but she was hungry, and the driver told her, "Eat! There is no other food here, and the journey is long."

So, Marisia recalled, "I forced myself to eat, and they actually tasted good." The truck brought them within walking distance of a railway station and a train trip directly back to Budapest.

When Hanka and Marisia arrived at one of the orphanages, Monek greeted them with a little three-year-old girl, also named Marisia, in his arms. Little Marisia's mother had asked to leave her with Monek for just a few weeks, while she traveled to Poland to find her younger child, a boy she had hidden with a family before she fled, but she was killed, apparently by a robber, leaving little Marisia an orphan.

Despite his compassion for all the children at the Budapest orphanages, my father always made an effort never to show favoritism, even toward my sister, Ewa. But for some reason, his emotional objectivity crumbled when he set eyes upon little Marisia. He wanted to adopt her, but Hela objected, feeling that Monek's attachment to the girl took attention away from the other children, in particular their own daughter. Fortunately the older Marisia had a reaction similar to my father's when she first saw little girl. The two Marisias became inseparable, the older girl taking it upon herself to be the younger one's nurse, mother, and big sister, while still only a teenager herself.

Little Marisia also had an adult guardian for a few months: Mila Riner, who had been at Auschwitz and had survived the camp with the help of Viola Török, a Hungarian Jewish doctor who had served as Mila's guardian angel while Mila fought illness.[7] When Mila got to Budapest, she heard about this house with people from Poland, children, and a kitchen providing hot meals. She arrived at the house with a friend named Chaycia, with whom she had shared a barrack in Auschwitz.

Mila originally was from Tarnów, and she and Hela bonded. She and Chaycia were watching the new arrivals daily, with the hope that Chaycia's fiancee, Paweł, would appear. Hela empathized with Mila, who was depressed over the loss of her entire family, and with Chaycia, who presumed she had lost her sweetheart. Hela encouraged both not to lose hope. Things would get better for them, she said. Lo and behold, as one reads only in fairy tales, one sunny day, Pawel wandered into the house, looking for the hot soup, available to new arrivals, that he had heard about. Paweł Owide and Chycia soon married.

Shortly afterwards, my mother introduced Mila to my uncle Aron

---

7   Dr. Viola Török and her husband, Dr. Gabriel Török, later immigrated to Israel and worked at the Malben Hospital, Beer Yaakov, which my father directed. Later they became two of the founders of the Ben Gurion University Medical School.

Osterweil. When he finally made it out of Siberia, Aron arrived at one of the houses without even knowing that Dr. Kotarba, who ran the place, was really his brother Monek. Eventually Aron and Mila, too, got married there in Budapest.

My uncle Ushier also survived and found his way back to Budapest. Ewa saw him arrive and still remembers the great pleasure of being the one to reunite him with his wife, Hanka.

Eventually, an adoptive family was found for little Marisia. Dr. Klapholz and his wife, whom my father knew from Poland, provided her with love and affection, a comfortable home, and an excellent education. Unfortunately, they neglected to tell her about her past; she learned about her early childhood from the recruiter at the draft office when she joined the Israeli armed forces at the age of 18. It took many years for her to forgive her parents for keeping the truth from her.

One of the connections my father developed in Budapest was a Russian colonel who happened to be Jewish and was sympathetic to the plight of the refugees. The colonel was a lover of fine timepieces, so Monek bought watches for him from local pawn shops. The colonel, in turn, helped Monek find more food and medication for the children. The colonel also reminded my father that even after the liberation of Hungary, there was still reason for caution. "You should really leave here," he advised Monek one day. "It may not be such a great place to live under Russian control."

The colonel knew that his own troops had drastically reduced the ability of anyone in Hungary to leave. The trains normally scheduled for other locations from Budapest never seemed to leave on time and were sometimes cancelled. The Russians forced Hungarian men to build pontoon bridges, so that both halves of the city could be reunited. They also transferred approximately 600,000 people to Soviet labor camps, where an estimated 200,000 Hungarians died under brutal conditions.

My father started making arrangements to move the children from Budapest to West Germany, which was controlled by Allied forces. The ultimate goal was to get them to Palestine, but even their evacuation to West Germany was complicated. Eventually it was determined that they would be transported in two main groups. First the Polish children would go, largely under the supervision of Monek, and later the Hungarian children would follow them. Many people assisted in this undertaking, including emissaries from the Zionist movements in Hungary and some who came from Palestine to assist in organizing the *bricha*, the Hebrew term then in use for the escape from the Iron Curtain of Soviet dominance that was descending on Eastern Europe. The influence and financial support of the American Joint Distribution Committee (AJDC) and Zionist underground organizations, in particular Hashomer Hatzair, also helped make the escape possible.

Most of the children traveled in groups by train. On the train platform in Budapest one day during this process, my mother told my father that she recognized an emissary from Palestine whom she met earlier in Budapest. My mother's vision was notoriously bad, and the woman was standing a significant distance away, bundled in heavy winter clothing, but my mother thought she recognized her from the way she stood and moved. My father doubted my mother was right, but she insisted.

"Rachel!" my mother shouted. This was not the woman's real name, but it was the one by which my mother knew her. "Rachel" was an operative who had helped Jews escape from Eastern Europe to Palestine. She finally turned around, but she did not seem pleased as my parents moved toward her through the horde of waiting passengers. My mother identified herself and said that she knew Rachel from work she had done with people who passed through the children's houses in Budapest.

Rachel's intense gaze was defiant, not friendly. "What do you want?" Hela asked which way she was headed.

"I'm going east, to Warsaw," Rachel said. My mother asked her to try to find Jerzyk, who, Hanka had told her, was in an orphanage in Warsaw. Rachel promised to do her best, then disappeared into the crowd, leaving Monek doubting she would make good on her promise.

The children traveled by train to Prague via Bratislava. Their accommodations in Prague were like a camp, which upset many, especially the Hungarian children, who were not used to such living conditions. They were instructed not to speak Hungarian or Polish in public, to avoid being recognized by the Soviets as foreigners. The children were very anxious to get out of Prague. Expectations and rumors led some to believe that they would be going by train to England and from there flying to Palestine. In fact, their route to Palestine would be far more complicated. Monek, by turns stern and calming, tried to put them at ease, reassuring them that no matter what route they took, he would support them and see that they were fed, clean, and safe.

The next step was to move the children from Soviet-occupied Prague to a displaced persons (DP) camp in Bamberg, Germany, which was under U.S. control. My parents were supposed to bring the first group, but then my mother was stricken with cellulitis and lymphangitis in her arm. The arm was red and painful, and she had swollen lymph nodes, which made it hard for her to function. While not life-threatening in itself, the condition could have seriously affected her if not treated properly. Ironically, it was a German doctor in Prague who treated her with sulfa medication. Her friend from home, Yda, who had also joined them in Budapest, volunteered to stay with Hela and keep her company until Monek could come and fetch her, once her infection had resolved. Monek and Ewa went on ahead with the children, leaving Hela lonely and anxious in Prague, without much news about the progress of the others.

One day, in January 1946, about a week or so after Monek and the children had left for Bamberg, Hela was staring out the window and saw something unusual: a young boy, wearing a long winter coat and high boots, trudging through the snow directly toward Hela's apartment. As he moved closer, even though his face was not clear, my mother knew that it was Jerzyk. She had not had high hopes that her conversation with the woman on the train platform would bear fruit, but there he was, shivering, pale, emaciated — but alive. She brought him inside, gave him soup and tea, and listened as he told her what had happened to him.

On September 2, 1943, the Germans had assembled the ghetto Jews once again in the Rynek plaza of Tarnów, separating the men from the women and selecting Jews to be taken away. Jerzyk held onto his mother, my aunt Faiga, huddled with the women on one side. When aunt Faiga's name was called out, she looked at Jerzyk and told him to run to his father on the other side of the plaza. Jerzyk tried protesting so she sternly repeated her instructions, "Run to Daddy. Run!" Somehow he managed to get across the plaza in full view of the German soldiers, with their guns drawn, to his father, my uncle Herman. He never saw his mother again.

Jerzyk knew that his mother had died, but only in recent years did his research reveal that the train she was put on was headed for

Auschwitz. Looking back on those moments, Jerzyk equated himself to Bambi, the deer in the Disney movie whose mother sacrifices her own life to save her child. The pain and anger he feels whenever he thinks of his mother's fate touches me deeply.

Young Jerzyk followed his father to work at Madritsch's Tarnów factory. When they learned that an inspection by the Nazis was about to take place, Jerzyk hid with another boy, Marcel Tesse, under a desk in a factory office. That night, they slept in the factory, behind huge rolls of fabric, near the watchful eyes of Mrs. Tesse.

Two days later, Jerzyk, hiding under my uncle's long winter coat, marched again from the ghetto gate into the factory. My uncle Herman took Jerzyk out to the porch of the building and introduced him to a young Polish woman, Joanna (Janka) Tecko.[8] He told Jerzyk to use the last name Ostrovski and to go with Joanna.

Joanna took him by train to Warsaw and delivered him to his mother's niece, Ziuta Lamensdorf, who was older and had escaped from Tarnów by using false papers, changing her name to the more Polish-sounding Elżbieta Brodzianka in the process. The two women were linked by the Polish Communist underground, and Elżbieta was the one who had requested Janka's assistance. When Ziuta saw him, though she must have expected his arrival, she said, "What am I going to do with you now," a common Polish expression of anguish and caring. Jerzyk spent the night, but, since it was not safe enough there, he was sent with Joanna the following morning to a Polish family, also connected to the underground, on the outskirts of Warsaw.

---

8   For a brief report of Joanna Tecko's saving of Herman and Jerzyk Osterweil and her inclusion in Yad Vashem's Righteous Among the Nations, see Klara Jackl, "Story of Rescue — Tecko Joanna," August 2021. https://sprawiedliwi.org.pl/en/stories-of-rescue/story-rescue-tecko-joanna, retrieved 11/18/2021.

Joanna came every couple of weeks to take Jerzyk for a short visit with his cousin. On one such visit, Jerzyk was surprised by the presence of his father, who had managed to escape, with the help of false documents provided by Joanna, before the Tarnów ghetto liquidation. They were able to spend several hours together, but then Jerzyk was taken back to the family he was hiding with, while Uncle Herman was placed by the underground with a family named Karpiński. Joanna accompanied the boy as they traveled to and from his father's apartment for occasional visits, but Herman felt it was safer for young Jerzyk to live in a separate location.

One day, when Jerzyk was preparing to visit his father at the Karpińskis, an unexpected visitor arrived: a young man who claimed to be a doctor. After a hushed conversation with the woman of the house, the young doctor emerged and declared that Jerzyk was sick, without even examining him. "You need to rest in bed," the young doctor declared. "You cannot visit your father. First, you must get healthy." With that, the man left as abruptly as he had arrived.

The next weekend, Jerzyk was allowed to visit his father, and he told him what had happened. Herman decided to keep Jerzyk with him, instead of sending him back with Joanna to the house where he had been staying, but he would not explain why.

A few days later, on February 25, 1944, just over a year before Jerzyk arrived at my mother's apartment, the doorbell rang at the Karpińskis' apartment. Only my uncle Herman and Jerzyk were there at the time. Jerzyk remembered seeing his father look downstairs from a window, recognize one of the visitors, and press a buzzer to allow them entrance to the building.

At the front door of the apartment, four men appeared. One of them was the young doctor who had previously declared Jerzyk too sick to travel. They took my uncle Herman into the Karpińskis' bedroom. Jerzyk heard an intense exchange behind the closed door, including what sounded like a demand for money.

His suspicion was confirmed when one of the four men emerged and cut open every shoe sole in the hallway closet, looking for hidden valuables. Finding none, they kept Herman in the bedroom, separated from his son. Late in the afternoon, Mr. and Mrs. Karpiński returned home, only to be angrily interrogated by the men in the dining room. The Karpińskis insisted that they had no hidden money or other items in the apartment.

Eventually, the four men gave up their inquisition of the Karpińskis, but they dragged Herman out of the bedroom into the hallway. His overcoat was already on, and the four men were about to force him to leave with them. Jerzyk, panicked, called out to his father, "Daddy, wait! I am getting my coat! I'm coming with you!"

Herman barked angrily at the boy, "No! You stay here!" Jerzyk, not fully understanding the situation, was still determined to go with his father. He went to the closet to get his coat, and as he did, he heard what sounded like a shattered light bulb. It was a gun shot. Herman slid to the floor, blocking the front door. Two of the men pulled Herman's body by the hem of his coat to the center of the hallway, and then the four left.

The Karpińskis could not go to the Warsaw police. Instead, they contacted the underground police, those who secretly intervened to help the underground resolve crimes that could not be reported to the authorities. Jerzyk had to sleep that night in the bed he had been sharing with his father, while the door to the hallway remained open, his father's body still lying there.

Very early the next morning, Mrs. Karpiński took Jerzyk by the hand through the snowy streets of Warsaw to Jerzyk's cousin, Ziuta. When Ziuta first laid eyes on him and heard what happened from

Mrs. Karpiński, she reacted as she had before. "What am I going to do with you?" She had to find a new family to place him with.

Joanna Tecko took Jerzyk to another hiding place on the western edge of Warsaw, the small home of an older Polish widow. There, Joanna regularly visited him and brought greetings and small gifts from Ziuta. The widow, in an effort to keep Jerzyk as safe as possible, began taking the boy to church so no one would be aware of his Jewish heritage. He was not inspired by church ceremonies but found the incense pleasing.

Jerzyk's most cherished possession, boots that he got from his father while in the ghetto, desperately needed repair. Despite the holes in the soles, however, Jerzyk refused to part with the boots, as they were a special gift from his father. He would send messages to his cousin Ziuta asking for the money to repair them, not fully comprehending the financial difficulty Ziuta was in, just like the rest of the occupied population. Eventually Ziuta came through anyway, and Jerzyk wore those repaired boots the day he met Hela in Prague.

Despite the loss of his father and the dangers surrounding him, Jerzyk was one of the fortunate ones. No one pointed a finger at the elderly widow and the boy who had begun living with her, and he was able to witness the Soviet takeover of Warsaw, Russian troops marching west on a main boulevard close to the widow's house. Within a couple of days, Ziuta showed up in a horse-drawn carriage and took him to Otwock, a village where a Jewish organization had opened an orphanage for surviving Jewish children. In the orphanage, he was frequently visited by Ziuta, who was then wearing the uniform of a lieutenant in the Polish army, a pistol holstered on her hip.

The children at the orphanage in Otwock were enrolled in a local Polish school and instructed by a visiting rabbi in Jewish studies. Jerzyk finally felt safe there, but then he developed a fever. His neck began to swell, and a hacking cough followed. He was finding it hard to breathe. He had contracted diphtheria at a time and place when there were no antibiotics available to treat it, so he was kept in isolation for quite a long time.

It was during Jerzyk's battle with diphtheria that lists of Polish survivors were published and circulated in various locations, to help families separated by the events of the war. (Such efforts continued on a diminishing scale well into the 1960s.) Hanka spotted Jerzyk's name on one of those lists. She tried to get him out so he could join her on the trip back to Budapest, but the medical authorities would not let the boy out of quarantine.

The Russian presence meant that there was no official way to get out of the country. Jerzyk would have to be secretly guided across the border. Toward the end of 1945, after Jerzyk had recovered from diphtheria, he was approached one day by two young men who were clearly foreign but spoke perfect Polish. These men belonged to the same organization as Rachel, the operative Hela had seen in the railroad station in Budapest. They told Jerzyk that his aunt Hela sent them to get him out of Poland. He went with them by train to the southern Polish border and then walked with him into Czechoslovakia. They joined a group of about a hundred other Jews posing as Greeks seeking repatriation, and they crossed the Tatra Mountains between Slovakia and Poland on foot.

The entire group survived the freezing snow of the Tatra Mountains. When their new names as Greek refugees were read at the border checkpoint, each person in the group responded with "ken," meaning *yes* in Hebrew. The border guards thought they spoke Greek. Once inside Czechoslovakia, Jerzyk and the two men who took him from Otwock boarded a train to Prague, where he arrived and astonished my mother.

When he had recounted the whole tale to Hela, Jerzyk told her, "I think the man who said he was the doctor blocked my visit with my father. I think he tried to get money from us to help us escape." It was a common nightmare, and my family had heard of such stories in Tarnów. Herman had likely given an agreed-upon amount that the four men decided was not enough; they were planning to rob him of further money, and did not want the boy present. Jerzyk never figured out how the escape was planned or who put his father in contact with those men. Years later, Ziuta told Jerzyk that those same men revisited the apartment and murdered Mr. Karpiński. For years, Jerzyk had flashbacks of that day. He also had the same kind of survivor's guilt that plagued Marisia. "Maybe if I had insisted on going to visit him the week before," he said, more than once, "I could have warned him that that 'doctor' was up to something, and my father would have survived."

CHAPTER 11

Caring for the Displaced

On New Year's Eve, as 1945 became 1946, Monek began moving the children from Czechoslovakia to the American-occupied zone of Germany. The plan was for the children to hide in the backs of trucks, with tarpaulins preventing anyone from easily seeing the human cargo. Between New Year celebrations and the bitter cold, Monek and the other staff gambled that the Soviet guards at the Czech border would be fortified with drink when the trucks rolled up to their outpost, and that they would not ask too many questions.

The gamble paid off, but the next part of the trip had to be on foot, in knee-high snow. The children took turns carrying Monek's rounded, doctor's briefcase. Ewa recalls stopping for the night in a cow shed, where one of the youngsters screamed as something warm fell on her head. It was cow manure. Finally, they made it to a train that would take them the rest of the way to Bamberg.

Bamberg was an ironic place, historically, for the young refugees to find haven. In 1926, Adolf Hitler had convened the Bamberg Conference to create unity within the then-new Nazi Party. Bamberg was chosen because the faction that disagreed with Hitler was centered in that area of Franconia, in the north, but it was still not far from Bavaria and the Hitler supporters.

A disturbing historical footnote suggests the unwillingness of Bamberg's remaining Hitler loyalists to acknowledge the end of the war. Toward the end of fighting, a nineteen-year-old student in Bamberg, Robert Limpert, tried to convince the town to surrender to the Allied forces without further military resistance. Betrayed by local members of the Hitler Youth, and by order of Bamberg's military commander, Colonel Ernst Meyer, the young student was hanged from the portal of the city hall. It was just days before the war ended.

Bamberg itself, first mentioned in historical texts in the year 902, was most attractive in appearance, situated over seven sloping hills. But the DP camp was far from welcoming. The children were treated with DDT to delouse them. There were two main buildings, both very crowded. One building had rooms where the children slept. The other building was where they were treated and fed. The buildings had been used by the military prior to their being used for displaced persons, or DPs.

For two years after the end of the war, about 850,000 people lived in DP camps, mainly in Germany, Austria, and Italy. The United Nations Relief and Rehabilitation Agency (UNRRA) was responsible for running the camps, along with the military of the country that controlled the zone where the camp was located. At Bamberg, the American military shared control with the UNRRA. By August of that year, Bamberg would house nearly 3,000 refugees.

Still, the children at the DP camp were finally truly safe, and their living conditions were better than they had been in Prague. Something as simple as having hot water for bathing was a huge boost to their spirits. There were problems, however. My father sent a letter to Hashomer Hatzair headquarters in Munich complaining of broken toilets and insufficient facilities for washing. (The Zionist movements provided assistance in addition to that obtained from UNRRA.) He wrote that there was not enough space for all the children, and that the food they were served was not good enough in quality or quantity, especially given the level of malnourishment many of the children had already suffered. He worried that they would fall ill.

Part of the problem was that many people throughout post-war Germany lived under highly adverse conditions. The food available in Bamberg was limited and often spoiled. The doctors who saw the children tried their best to keep them healthy, but limited medicine and no money for proper equipment hampered their efforts.

Bamberg was a mere 60 miles from Nuremberg, where the trials of former Nazi officials were concluding in 1946. Soviet, British, American, and French judges, in a military tribunal, meted out punishment to two dozen men, including Martin Bormann, Rudolf Hess, and Hermann Göring. A minority of them expressed repentance for their involvement in the Holocaust. The German population was equally reluctant to acknowledge its complicity — and now they had a camp full of children, most of them Jewish, living in their district, to remind them of the things that they desperately wanted to forget.

Before dawn on his ninth birthday, January 9, 1946, my cousin Jerzyk arrived with other refugees at the Bamberg camp. After hours of being processed, completing paperwork, being cleaned and sprayed with DDT, and receiving new clothes, he stood in line for his daily food rations. Jerzyk remembers the seductive smell of freshly baked white bread, which was not available in Poland. Each person received a loaf of bread while waiting in line for other food. By the time Jerzyk arrived at the beginning of the line, he had already devoured his entire bread ration for the day. Jerzyk was then directed to the building where the children and administrators slept. He trudged up a stairway to join the others, but he stopped before reaching the top. There was my sister Ewa, whom he recognized, even though the last time he had seen her was five years before, when he was merely four years old. Used to upheaval in their young lives, they chatted in an almost casual way, neither becoming emotional about what they had been through.

Jerzyk continued up the stairs and entered a room where he saw four men, all staff members at the camp, still in bed. Although he had recognized Ewa, he could not tell which man was my father. He timidly identified himself and then asked which one of them was Monek. My father sat up in bed and opened his arms to his nephew, who was now finally safe. Jerzyk would become so integral a part of my family that I consider him my brother.

My father and others worked hard to obtain better conditions for the children, and before long they were moved to a different location, in Strüth, near the northern border of the Ansbach district in Bavaria. Compared to Bamberg, the new camp's structure and physical location were a marked improvement. It had previously been a sanatorium for those who needed medical treatment and rest for tuberculosis. Jerzyk and Ewa and the other children were wide-eyed as they beheld the grounds at Strüth for the first time. The grounds were well kept and included an orchard with fruit trees and vegetable and flower gardens, with a forest to the west of the buildings where my mother and sister would take long walks in the coming weeks and months. There was plentiful food, supplemented by fresh local produce in season. After all the children had been through, it must have seemed like a paradise on Earth.

My sister and Jerzyk fit in well with the other children. My father made sure never to show favoritism toward either one of them, so that no children would feel jealous or vengeful or worry that they did not matter. Monek was not just a doctor and administrator but also an educator and a father figure. A school was set up, and the teaching was done in Hebrew. Jerzyk remembers that on the first day of school, his teacher, Mr. Klag, asked the students to introduce themselves to the class. When Jerzyk announced his name, Mr. Klag said, softly, "There is no equivalent for your name in Hebrew, so we'll call you Josef." He has been known by that name from that day forth.

Struth became the best experience for these children since their pre-war lives with their families in their home countries. My father tended to the children's health with great care, pleased to see their skin clearing, their malnourished bodies filling out, and the occasional smiles appearing on their faces. He enjoyed spending time with them. Ewa recalls my father sitting on a bench on a small hill, surrounded by children who sat on the grass listening to him read the story of Robinson Crusoe, translating from German to Polish as he read. The children grew healthier and began to have a semblance of normality in their lives.

There were some exceptions. A boy named Julek Czoban contracted rheumatic fever and then developed pericarditis. The accumulation of fluid had to be drained, to relieve pressure on the heart and alleviate chest pain and shortness of breath. My father took him to a nearby hospital and performed a pericardiocentesis, a draining of the fluid using a needle inserted through the chest wall. This kind of procedure can be risky: the needle can trigger a rhythm abnormality of the heart if it touches the heart muscle. Monek did not have the benefit of the medical instruments we use today to perform this procedure, but he was determined to help this child, and he carefully extracted the fluid without any ultrasound to guide him. That was only one example of his determination and skill as a pediatrician in less-than-ideal circumstances.

My father was also very concerned about Shlomo Arad, who with his brother had spent so much time on the streets in Budapest. Despite the plentiful food at Strüth, Shlomo was still so emaciated and malnourished that Monek insisted he be transferred to the hospital in Ansbach "to fatten him up." His body had been leached of nutrients and he needed the additional care.

Shlomo, however, did not want to leave his brother, the staff, or the other children at Strüth. He was brought to the hospital despite his protests, but he hated it so much that after a few days he turned his pajamas inside out, threw on a coat and shoes, and walked all the way back to Strüth. It was decided that if Shlomo was healthy enough to do that, he didn't belong in the hospital any longer.

Monek never really lost his temper, but he did at times get frustrated. Sometimes, he would walk among the children, asking insistently, "What about my book?" He wanted books that the children had borrowed to be returned to him. The children knew he wasn't really as angry as he seemed, and that he was happy they were reading and learning. Ewa and Shlomo described him to me as projecting confidence: when the children felt fear or concern about their future, he reassured them, saying that he would use his own money to ensure their comfort, no matter where they all wound up living.

My father's real frustration came from his disagreements with some of the other adults who took an interest in the fate of the children. Since they left Budapest, the children had been in two main groups. One group, consisting mostly of Polish children, was under Monek's care. The other group, of primarily Hungarian children, was overseen by a man named Moshe Laufer. Other children had come along later, under the auspices of the Jewish Agency. There was no clear designation of who was in charge of the children, and along with my father and Laufer, a man named Zvi Langzman also claimed some authority.

The crux of the problem was that the children were caught up in the turmoil of the founding of the state of Israel. There were many competing ideas about the shape the new country would take, and my father, Laufer, and Langzman disagreed about how these children would fit in. My father wanted to establish a pioneering settlement, run according to Socialist ideals, with at least some of the children. He felt that would be the best way he could fulfill the vow he had made that day in Janowska. Laufer and Langzman opposed him, saying that the children belonged to the whole nation and should not be recruited to one ideology, but they often disagreed with each other as well. "He thought my work was an obstacle to his goals," my father wrote of Laufer. "And he fought with me, the same as he fought with Zvi Langzman."

Since there was no agreement as to who was in charge of the children, Laufer went ahead and organized activities for physical education and the study of Hebrew. He also insisted that all the children be part of *kibbutzim*, working on projects at the camp, presumably in preparation for being sent to Palestine. Activists were brought into the camp to assist in this indoctrination. Other Zionist leaders would also visit.

In his writings, my father discussed going with Langzman to Munich to present their disagreements to the Hashomer Hatzair leadership there. Monek insisted that Langzman and the other Zionist leaders "were not an organic part of our movement." Langzman, for this part, did not recognize Monek as either an authority or a responsible party in the struggle to control the destiny of the children. "The children belong to the whole nation," Langzman said to those at the presentation in Munich, referring to them almost as property of the future state of Israel. Langzman went on to declare that the Jewish Agency, which was more nationalistic and global, would settle Israel without any of the youth movements that Monek preferred.

After their return from Munich, Monek condemned Langzman even more aggressively in writing. "His instructions are anti-democratic and fascist. We ourselves will take care of the affairs of the kids. Who gave them permission to disregard and disrespect the youth movement?" But my father was fighting a losing battle. Shlomo Arad claims that most of the children had faith that Monek would take the best care of them. His ideas included giving them much more freedom and independence. The leadership of Hashomer Hatzair, however, was dead set against Monek's plan. In early 1947, they decided that all the children would be taken away from Strüth to be raised on *kibbutzim* in Palestine.

My father was devastated. Ewa, without knowing then what the problem was, recalls seeing him walking with our mother in the forest in Strüth in a very grim mood. He had turned down earlier opportunities to emigrate with all our family to Palestine or the United States, wanting to make *aliyah* with the children from Budapest and establish a settlement according to his pioneering ideals. He understood these kids. He knew what they needed and how to provide for those needs. He wanted to support them further and help them adjust in the new land. Now the decision had been taken away from him, and his plans would never reach fruition. It was a bitter pill for him to swallow.

CHAPTER 12

Refugees and Reunions

I was born April 10, 1947, in Bleidorn, a refugee camp, also in the Ansbach district, where my father had become medical director of the hospital and pediatric ward. My family spent my first four years in refugee camps.

Bleidorn had been a German military base and had a huge plaza, where they had conducted exercises and training before its conversion to a DP camp. It had four main buildings, two at the eastern border of the property and two at the western edge. To the north was what served as an auditorium and gymnasium, so the children at the camp could have a place to exercise and play. The school and administrative building were to the south, and near the auditorium was the main gate to the camp, where a ramp led to the other structures. There was a hospital in one of the main buildings, and a canteen. Refugees from Russia and Poland set up a bakery making traditional breads. They also used the oven to make *cholent*, a Jewish Sabbath dish of slowly baked meat, vegetables, and beans, prepared on Friday and cooked overnight. Overall conditions were good there, although it did not have the beauty of Strüth.

The Jews of Northern Europe, despite their many different languages, could always communicate in Yiddish, and that was the main language spoken at the camp. In the elementary school where Ewa and Jerzyk studied, however, all classes were conducted in Hebrew, with multiple classes studying Hebrew at various levels of ability. My mother, fluent in Hebrew from her Hebrew school and Hashomer Hatzair days, became a Hebrew teacher there.

There were other courses as well, some of them preparing the children for future vocations. Jerzyk took a class in electronics. Years later, he told me that it was less than satisfactory. "They taught practical things, like how to care for a battery," Jerzyk complained, "but not how it works." But Jerzyk's curiosity in that course at Bleidorn shaped his future: he eventually became an electrical engineer.

The school emphasized all Jewish holidays and the development of the new Jewish state. Ewa participated in drawing a mural depicting the map of the country of Israel. The boy who led the effort later folded it carefully to take it with him on his voyage there. Once, before the holiday of Purim, the children were making masks as a school activity. Ewa and Jerzyk got the idea to make a bird mask from a movie they saw in town. In the movie, the hero poured plaster on the face of his dead beloved. Ewa had some experience with plaster from having her arm put in a cast. Julek, the child on whom my father had performed a pericardiocentesis, was their model. They covered his face with gauze, poured plaster on it, and waited for it to harden. When it dried, they painted it. The mask looked so realistic that when they showed up in my room with it, I was terrified. They also tried to place it on my face. The smell of the fresh plaster is a vivid memory to this very day. From that day forward, every time I misbehaved, they just had to say, "Be good — or else Purim is coming!"

When the State of Israel was declared, in May, 1948, there was a day-long celebration at the camp, a day Ewa and Jerzyk remember as full of joy. It was followed by music and dancing, including the traditional *horah*, that stretched far into the night. But the Jews and Arabs of Palestine were already at war when the State was declared; that day, the armies of the surrounding Arab countries invaded. The following day saw stations put up at the camp for recruitment into the Israeli Defense Force. Sentiment ran high that every able-bodied person should volunteer for the army, and those who refused were ostracized. Some people posted the names of those who refused to sign up in black frames, as if they were deceased.

It was at Bleidorn that we were finally reunited with my mother's brother Fredek Ladner, who had been in Siberia with David Ladner and Aron Osterweil. His wife, Herta, had died at Belzec in 1943, but he survived and returned to Germany, where he had lived before being deported by the Nazis in 1938. Knowing that Hela wanted to spend more time teaching, he introduced her to Erika Marten, the sister of one of his acquaintances in Ludenscheid, and Erika became my nanny or *au pair*.

Fredek's love of children was evident. His purchase of a violin for Jerzyk made a major impact on the boy. Jerzyk's father, Herman, had played the violin very well, and there were expectations that Jerzyk might have a similar talent. Fredek also bought Ewa and Jerzyk their first bicycle, not a simple task in those days, when most German factories were not producing consumer items. The bike had a tendency to break apart after each ride, but Jerzyk, with his technical ingenuity, managed to fix it. He had to improvise a great deal, as spare parts were not available. Fredek also gave Jerzyk a drill and wires and had the boy help him build cords for irons. Something as simple as an iron was not commercially available as a new item in post-war Germany. Once Jerzyk put them together, Fredek was able to sell the irons.

Another gift from Uncle Fredek contributed a great deal to some of the nicer moments we enjoyed during the Bleidorn DP camp period: a genuine leather soccer ball. The children were overjoyed to be playing with a real ball instead of one made out of rags. Ewa recalls getting castor oil from our father to apply to the leather to safeguard this treasured item.

Fredek did not have much formal education, but he was a very intuitive and practical person. Years later, during my medical studies in Siena, Italy, he showed up one day carrying a basket filled with all kinds of goodies, including not only apples, pears, and chocolates but pineapple, which was rare and expensive in Europe. He apologized for not bringing flowers, but he said, "I figured that, for you students, what's in that basket will serve you better than flowers."

Another person my father was able to help was Franz Fritsch, who had led my family out of Poland. Monek was able to arrange for a generous grant from the AJDC to help Fritsch rehabilitate himself economically. Fritsch was able to use the funds to build a guest house in a village near the Austrian border, and my family often visited him there. During their visits, Fritsch invited Ewa for walks along the riverbank, which was the border between Germany and Austria, and told her to pick up any packages that she might see lying on the riverbank. My mother once saw Ewa returning to the house, carrying a sack full of coffee bags. When Hela confronted Fritsch, he admitted he was smuggling the coffee. Fritsch also once asked Jerzyk to stand guard on a hill and light a cigarette whenever he saw anyone getting close to the riverbank where smugglers crossed with rowboats. Fritsch was never one to ignore an opportunity.

My father, on the other hand, was always trying to find ways to help more people, knowing how weakened the Bleidorn population had been from starvation, stress, and infectious disease. In addition to his work as a pediatrician and setting up the nursing school, he also set up a clinic to screen the local population for infectious diseases and other manageable illnesses, a preventive health care approach that was far ahead of its time.

My father's focus at Bleidorn went beyond the immediate medical needs of the patients. Bent on helping to create a workforce for the nascent nation of Israel, he opened a nursing school at Bleidorn under the auspices of ORT, an acronym in Russian for Association for the Promotion of Skilled Trades. Marisia Offen and Gusta Malinowski studied there to become nurses. Marisia served as my father's nurse assistant, a position she held for many years. She was later sent by my father to a nursing course in Switzerland to qualify as a pediatric nurse.

As people were repatriated and the camp population in Bleidorn diminished, Monek was approached by Dr. Boris Pliskin, a representative of the American Joint Distribution Commission (AJDC) in Munich, and asked to take the role of chief physician and medical director of a Jewish refugee hospital there. Bogenhausen Spital, as it was referred to in German, had been a girls' school. It was converted to a hospital after the war in April, 1946, to help the many people, Jews and non-Jews, who contracted tuberculosis or who were recovering from the various illnesses they had developed in concentration camps. In April, 1949, about the time we moved there, the hospital limited itself to Jewish patients.

We lived on the top floor, along with Gusta Malinowski and Marisia Offen, who were like members of our growing extended family. The building was not intended to house families, but the rooms were spacious and well-lit and heated during the cold winters in Munich. My father was allowed to bring in a few other refugees to work there with him. All workers, even part time, were allowed to live there.

During our time in Munich, both Ewa and Jerzyk went to a full-time Hebrew school about a mile away, on Mehlstrasse. They attended fifth and sixth grades there, studying a variety of subjects that included Latin and German. The studies were conducted according to the curriculum in Israel. They even had a visit from Baruch Oren, a superintendent from the Israeli Ministry of Education, who gave Ewa an issue of *Davar Le-Yeladim*, a children's magazine published in Israel.

While my father was careful about unnecessary spending, on clothing in particular, he would spare no expense on culture and education. In Munich, he insisted on sending Ewa and Jerzyk to the opera. He bought a subscription that could be shared with friends and colleagues. He loved Italian operettas and operas by Franz Lehár, Jacques Offenbach, and others, and he amassed quite a collection of records. He loved classical music, especially Beethoven.

In the summer of 1949, he sent Ewa and Jerzyk to a summer camp sponsored by OSE (*Oeuvre de Secours aux Enfants* or Children's Aid Society). They spent six weeks in Champéry, in the western, French-speaking part of Switzerland, where they had breathtaking alpine views. My mother sometimes took Ewa on vacations to beautiful places such as the spa town of Bad Reichenhall and Lake Koenigssee, and Monek took Jerzyk on trips as well. It was very different from life during the war.

My father felt that his position carried not only medical responsibility but social responsibility. Many people looked to him to organize events. He looked for any opportunity to bring joy to the hospital patients. He made sure that all Jewish holidays were celebrated. He lent his turntable and records to communal dance parties. We had a private family Purim party where he even danced himself, surprising my sister, who had never seen him dance before.

(To the best of my knowledge, we never saw him dance again.)

When my father was asked to take over, Bogenhausen Spital was in disarray, fraught with management dysfunction and patient complaints about the German doctors who dominated the hospital staff. The Munich hospital had many Jewish survivors of the Holocaust as patients, and my father was committed to seeing that they did not experience any undue stress after their war experiences. When he took over the job as medical director, he examined the records of the doctors who worked there. In a number of cases, he found doctors who carried cards as active members of the Nazi party during the war. He felt that cast a shadow on their credentials, and that Holocaust survivors should not have to be subjected to Nazi doctors. He dismissed those doctors from the staff.

This set off a firestorm of debate. It reached a pinnacle when one Munich newspaper carried a front-page article attacking Monek, even referring to him as a "Jüdische Nazi," a Jewish Nazi. This absurdity infuriated my father, and only intensified his determination to stick to his decision. The American military police, who had ultimate control over the security of the hospital, placed a great deal of trust in my father and supported his recommendations. Despite the public sentiment against him, the dismissed doctors were not rehired.

Thinking back on the stories I have heard, I am amazed at how my father handled crises. No matter how bad the situation was, he was able to deal with his grief and frustration and charge forward with a new plan.

Monek stayed at the Bogenhausen Jewish Hospital for two years, until it closed. He had no trouble finding another job. He was recruited, without going through a formal search process, to be medical director of the Malben Hospital in Be'er Ya'akov, Israel, a five hundred–bed TB hospital that was under construction. (Based on correspondence between Charles Passman, head of the AJDC, Israel, and Samuel L. Haber, director of the AJDC in Germany and Austria, Monek's appointment was rather unusual, and relied on his track record and the endorsements he received from his time at Bogenhausen.) Monek decided to take the position, so, in May of 1951, we left our life of alpine vacations and strolls in the parks of Munich and headed for the still-new State of Israel.

CHAPTER 13

A New Life in Israel

May 6, 1951, the day we boarded the *SS Artza*, bound for Israel, was Ewa's thirteenth birthday. She later said that seeing the ship's name, written in Hebrew letters — *Artza* means "To the Land!" — and the blue and white Israeli flag on its mast was the best birthday present she had ever received. She was traveling with my parents, me, Jerzyk, and also Marisia and Gusta. We had driven together from Munich to Genoa, Italy, to meet the ship.

Uncle Fredek did not come with us. He had married Lilian, an American woman, and they went to live in the United States. I also had to say goodbye to Erika, my *au pair*, and to my friends in Munich, but I was looking forward to this new adventure.

During the voyage, my father attended to a number of patients who were hospitalized on the ship. One of them was Marisia. She had contracted a serious kidney disease while studying in Switzerland. He took turns with another doctor, together covering the unit 24 hours a day.

We arrived on May 15, 1951, at the port of Haifa. It was still dark outside. As we approached, the passengers crowded onto the deck, all excited to see the flickering lights of Haifa in the distance. After we finally docked, we were greeted by my mother's brother,

Oskar Ladner, who had lived there since the early 1930s, and by her sister Sala. They fought over who was going to host us, so we stayed first with Oskar in Tel Aviv, then with Sala in Petach Tikva. Since Oskar's apartment was very crowded, Jerzyk stayed initially with my uncle Ushier. Walking to Ushier's house, he was overwhelmed by the Hebrew lettering on the street signs and the passersby conversing in Hebrew, and even more overcome when he arrived at the house and was reunited with his cousins Avram and Olga. After all he had been through, he could hardly believe this was all real.

My father immediately started work at the Be'er Ya'akov Malben Hospital. Later renamed Shmuel Harofe Medical Center, it had been the first tuberculosis hospital in the Middle East. It had been built on the grounds of a British military camp, funded by Malben, an acronym for the Organization for the Care of Handicapped Immigrants. Malben was the Israeli subsidiary of the American Joint Distribution Commission, dedicated to health concerns within post-war Israel. Patients were housed in what used to be British army barracks, but with all-new, state-of-the-art equipment, much of it newly imported from the U.S. and the U.K.

My family was housed in the former barracks, in a string of rooms connected by an external covered walkway. Many structures on the grounds were dilapidated, with tin roofs. The area was fenced in with barbed wire and surrounded by citrus orchards. At night, we heard coyotes whining in the distance.

Near the main gate there was a big "transition town" (*maabara*), consisting of big tents or tin houses hastily built for hundreds of thousands of immigrants from Europe's DP camps and the Middle East, who rushed to Israel after the War of Independence. Many had been expelled from Arab countries such as Iraq, Syria, Libya, and Egypt, or left of their own accord in order to save themselves from an uncertain future in the wake of the war with Israel.

Sensitive to the plight of the many unemployed people in the *maabara*, Monek insisted on hiring as many of them as possible to work at the hospital, often against the objections of the top management at Malben. Many years later, as a doctor practicing in the same community, Ewa met some of the people Monek had helped by giving them employment or treating them pro bono, and she was the recipient of their deep gratitude. My father also volunteered as a consultant at the nearby Kibbutz Netzer Sereni. It had been founded by Holocaust survivors in 1948, and he made friends with several of the members. I remember that they sent him a sack of peanuts and invited all of us to swim in their pool, a great rarity and luxury in those days.

Antibiotic treatment for TB was in its infancy, but nutrition was a strong focus at Be'er Ya'akov. The hospital hired an excellent chef, who made sure that the patients and the staff had nutritious, hearty meals. I was fascinated by the electric tractor that carried food from an enormous kitchen to the various buildings. At that time, there was a recession in Israel, and food in the markets was by no means plentiful. People received rationed food using coupons supplied by the Office of Commerce. So my father, in additional to his medical duties, started a vegetable garden and saw to it that goats and chickens were raised on the grounds. He even encouraged the children to grow their own vegetables, setting aside a special section for them in the big garden. And he made sure to minimize waste, having leftover food from the kitchen used to feed the animals rather than thrown away. Hospital staff were entitled to three meals a day in the main dining hall. Some who commuted arranged their shifts so they would not miss breakfasts.

After two years, we moved to a house in Rishon Lezion, less than six kilometers from Be'er Ya'akov. Rishon Lezion, which means "first in Zion," had been founded as an agricultural settlement in 1882 by Jewish immigrants from Russia. It was, in fact, the second Jewish town to be built in Palestine outside of the walls of Jerusalem. Baron Edmond James de Rothschild brought agricultural advances to the area and founded the Carmel-Mizrahi Winery in 1886. David Ben-Gurion would be an active member of the labor union there on his way to becoming Israel's first prime minister. By the time we moved there, Rishon Lezion was a town of about 30,000 people.

In Rishon, we finally felt rooted. We had a single-family home surrounded by our own garden. We planted fruit trees, including a few that seemed exotic, such as the mango tree. We planted flowers in various colors. Monek brought animals to our backyard, including chickens, turkeys, and a dumb and very large German Shepherd mix. (I had little experience handling animals and was a bit scared of dogs. Jerzyk tried to help me overcome my fears by asking whether I would like to walk the dog on the leash. This turned out to be an unforgettable experience: the dog dragged me all over our back yard, leaving behind deep tracks in the soil and muddying my pullover.)

My mother used to deliver a tray of eggs whenever we visited our family in Tel-Aviv or Petach Tikva. The only casualty of this arrangement was poor Jerzyk, who had to get up every day at the crack of dawn to feed the animals before leaving for school. Our chickens and turkeys roamed free without incident until the German Shepherd helped himself to one of the birds. That was his last meal with us. We returned him to the family of one of the hospital drivers. We had a similar problem with two goats. I had a painting of a little goatherd with a flute hanging in my room, which inspired my father to surprise me with a baby goat for my birthday. Uncertain if the farmer would deliver the goat in time, he secured one from a different farmer, but then both showed up, so we kept both kids. As they grew, they started eating everything in sight, including our vegetable garden. My mother finally insisted that my father give them away.

I was used to thinking of my father as someone who spent a lot of time at the hospital and occasionally came home with a chicken, or a rabbit, or even a turtle. No one ever discussed the war, at least not in detail. Sometimes things happened, however, that convinced me that my family used to have more serious concerns than goats eating the vegetables. One example was a visit from Shlomo Arad. He was fully grown and healthy, wearing the uniform of a lieutenant in the Israeli Defense Forces, and I knew from the way they looked at each other, from the joy in my father's eyes and the gratitude in Shlomo's, that something important had passed between them, even if no one would explain to me what it was.

My father was by all accounts an excellent doctor, but he was no diplomat. If he felt strongly about something, he spoke out in no uncertain terms. He differed with the Malben management at Be'er Ya'akov on how to run the hospital, and they passed over him when he was in line to become head of pediatrics. He was certain he could effectively fulfill both roles, medical director and chief of pediatrics, but they disagreed. From there, the relationship deteriorated, and in November of 1955 he resigned.

Never one to let anything stop him, my father used his severance pay to support us while he went to Zurich for six months on a fellowship, studying developmental pediatrics. He returned full of new ideas, and soon he had opened a new practice in Tel Aviv, helping children with a wide variety of problems ranging from stuttering to Down syndrome. Three times a week, my father made the trip to the clinic, about 20 kilometers from our house in Rishon Lezion. My mother worked with him as a play therapist for the children. In Rishon Lezion, he had another pediatric clinic that was part of our house. It had a private entrance and was used for the care of babies and young children. Monek also asked Jerzyk, with his talent for electronic engineering, to help him create a device to accurately test the hearing of some of his patients with communication disorders. Today such devices are commonplace, but in Israel in the 1950s, none were available.

My father was very driven and very certain that he knew what was right. This allowed him to help many people, but it also caused friction, within the family as well as with colleagues. For example, I knew that Monek's relationship with his youngest brother, Ushier, was difficult, even though, as a child, I didn't understand why. I later learned that two of their worst points of conflict stemmed from their escape from Poland in 1943.

One element was that Ushier had paid most of the money for the family's escape, and he felt that Monek had never sufficiently compensated him for that. Rather than pay his brother back in cash, my father had sent a large container of furniture, including a piano and expensive equipment to Ushier in Tel Aviv, when we were still in Germany. Ushier thanked him for this gesture, and my father had no idea that his brother was actually harboring a deep resentment that his request for reimbursement had been ignored and replaced by something Monek decided was appropriate. There was never any direct confrontation over this, but Ushier developed a habit of not showing up to family events, including my sister Ewa's wedding.

The other issue concerned Franz Fritsch, who had guided our family to safety. Fritsch was a familiar name in our house. I remember my mother mentioning him, and how much she appreciated his gallantry and gentlemanly behavior all the way to freedom. He was a guest in our apartment during his many visits to Munich. Ushier had nominated Fritsch for the designation of Righteous Among the Nations, the honor bestowed by Yad Vashem on those gentiles who were heroic in assisting Jews during the Holocaust. The committee chair, a Supreme Court judge, requested that Monek sign a written declaration requesting that Fritsch be given the award. My father refused to sign, angering not only Ushier but my mother.

"Why can't you sign this?" Hela demanded to know. "Why are you being so stubborn?"

"No," my father insisted. "This honor is for people who risked their lives to save Jews without being paid for it. What Fritsch did, he did for money. That's not what the Righteous Among the Nations is about."

My mother pleaded with him, noting that while Fritsch was certainly paid, he risked his own life to guide us and others to safety. "He deserves to be commemorated," she told my father, firmly and loudly, but Monek would not relent. He had no ill will toward Fritsch. He had been happy to recommend him for the grant that allowed him to build that guest house in Germany, and he was grateful for the help Fritsch had provided, but he believed Fritsch did not qualify for this particular honor, and he remained steadfast in that belief.

About a year after this argument, at my father's birthday party in Rishon Lezion, we were all surprised when Uncle Ushier arrived. Not only did he show up for the party, but he also brought an uninvited guest. It was Franz Fritsch. Ushier was by then a prosperous maker of fine suits, and he had paid for Fritsch to travel from Germany for the occasion.

There were no harsh words exchanged, no hostile or suspicious glances. Cake and drinks were served, and everyone appeared warm and congenial. It almost seemed that all the old arguments were forgotten, until Fritsch turned to Monek and said, "Monek, why haven't you signed the recommendation for the award that the committee has requested?"

Monek didn't flinch. "Fritsch," he said calmly, "you are a wonderful human being. I am grateful for all you have done for us. But this award is meant for people who saved Jews without accepting payment. You, Fritsch, received money for that. So, as much as I am grateful, I stand by my refusal."

Fritsch nodded, smiled, and politely said, "I do understand your position, even though I disagree with you." They hugged and went back to the celebration, and no more was said between them about it. My mother felt bad about my father's stubborn refusal to endorse Fritsch to Yad Vashem's Righteous Among the Nations award.

Fritsch joined us at many other celebrations. My father even invited him once in Munich to celebrate the Passover Seder with us and the whole hospital staff. Monek simultaneously translated the proceedings into German so Fritsch could understand. He seemed to value Fritsch's friendship, but he never changed his mind about signing that document. My mother never understood his reasoning. That is why, every Christmas, she sent a crate of Jaffa oranges with a signed card to Fritsch in Germany.

One of Monek's contacts in Budapest, Rezső (Rudolf) Kasztner, would turn out to be one of the most controversial Jewish figures of the Holocaust period. Kasztner, as I noted above, had founded the Budapest Aid and Rescue Committee with Ottó Komoly, and had helped secure food for those in need through the American Joint Distribution Committee. During the German occupation, he had been in contact with various Nazi officials, and had developed a relationship as the chief negotiator with Adolf Eichmann, the infamous Nazi in charge of deportation of Jews to concentration camps. The deportations began happening at such an accelerated rate that Kasztner made a proposal that was unparalleled during the war.

He proposed to the Nazis that a trade be set up, later coldly referred to as "blood for goods." Negotiating with Eichmann and with Kurt Becher, who was in charge of the economic exploitation of Hungarian Jews, Kasztner proposed an exchange: spare the lives of 800,000 to one million Jews in Hungary, in exchange for 10,000 trucks being furnished to the Third Reich to be deployed on the eastern front. Because the Nazi war machine greatly needed the trucks, there was serious consideration of Kasztner's proposal, but it failed. Instead, Kasztner received permission to have a single train take Jews to freedom in Switzerland. In addition to this famous train Kasztner was involved in many other train smuggling activities.

Kasztner survived the War and became a spokesman for the Labor government's minister of trade and industry. But his fate, despite his efforts to save as many Hungarian Jews as possible, was bizarre, unpredictable, and tragic. Malkiel Gruenwald, a member of Mizrahi, the religious wing of the Zionist movement, who had lost most of his family in Hungary, self-published a newsletter calling Kasztner a collaborator and attacking him for negotiating with Eichmann. Israel's attorney general told Kasztner that, as a government official, he had to sue Gruenwald for libel or resign his government job.

The trial, in 1954–55, stunned the state of Israel. Instead of Gruenwald's having to defend his incendiary language, Kasztner was accused of not informing Jews during the war about what he knew of the extermination camps. The judge dismissed Kasztner's libel case, announcing that he had "sold his soul to the devil." This statement was quoted by major newspapers and tabloids and affects me to this day.

In March of 1957, while waiting to be cleared of being a Nazi collaborator, Kasztner was shot on the street near his home in North Tel-Aviv by members of a pre-state militia. In January of the following year, most of the previous judgement was overturned by the Supreme Court of Israel in a 4-to-1 decision. The Court found that the original judge had "erred seriously." One justice described Kasztner as "a man who exposed himself to mortal danger in order to save others."

My father and I discussed the events of those tumultuous days in Budapest during the libel trial of Rezső Kasztner against Malkiel Gruenwald in 1954–55 and the Eichmann trial in 1961. My father clearly believed that people maligned Kasztner because they did not understand the circumstances in those days. He had enormous respect for Kasztner and his organization, which had played an important role in my father's activities in Budapest during the War. My father's contacts in the Budapest Aid and Rescue Committee, Ottó Komoly and Hajnalka "Hansi" Brand, worked in Kasztner's office, and my father had been in constant contact with them to secure resources for the children under his care. Monek said that anyone who did anything to save Jews from death should get credit for it.

As he grew older, my father developed diabetes and coronary heart disease and had to slow down. My mother persuaded him to close the clinic in Tel Aviv and get a part-time salaried position. He assumed the job of municipality physician in Lod. In Israel, municipality physicians were assigned mostly indigent patients who had multiple chronic illnesses and were surviving primarily on public assistance, without access to mainstream medical care.

Monek developed a systematic approach to disease management, taking a proactive approach with those suffering from diabetes and heart disease. He added what could be called a "one-stop-shop" clinic for these elders. He provided the medical evaluation and management, and a lab technician drew their blood and performed tests within that same day, so Monek had their lab results and could adjust their medication. Having spent most of his life working with children, my father was now working very effectively as a geriatrician. My sister Ewa, who by then was a general practitioner in the Kupat Cholim Klalit, largest of Israel's health service organizations, substituted for him for a month and experienced the love and admiration the patients had for him. Some people may have found my father aggravating at times, but no one can deny that he left a huge legacy.

By the time I reached high school age, I decided I wanted to be a doctor as well. When I told my father that I had decided to go to medical school, he said, "We have to talk." He invited me into his sanctum, his study in the back of the house. It had a big, beautiful, heavy desk we bought in Germany, with two locked compartments on the sides and a drawer. On top, he had his pens, letter openers and scissor sets, all neatly organized. On the corner of the desk, he had a mushroom, painted in bright colors. On top of it, there was a bee. When you twisted the bee, a bell rang. He pulled out a small bottle of plum *slivovitz* that he made himself. This was a big honor. As we sat down, he poured two glasses and asked, "Why have you decided on going to medical school?"

I paused, caught off guard by the directness of his question. As he was sipping the liqueur, watching me put my thoughts together, I saw a subtle smile on his face. His brows were lifted in expectation. I started saying how much I admired his professional life and his dedication to children, and how I admired Ewa for going to general practice, a much harder role than a sub-specialist. "So, this why I want to follow in your footsteps, to help other people," I said. A big smile spread across his face. "Oh, good. I thought you were doing it for the money."

I took the exam to get into medical school, but it was so difficult that I did not make the cut. Wondering whether I could ever follow in the footsteps of my father, I went into military service in 1965, joining the infantry, but then switching to the Air Force, due to some back problems. The Air Force assigned me to a communication and encryption unit, where I eventually became the station commander. I thought long and hard about what direction to take in life at the conclusion of my three-year military service, but the answer quickly became clear. My father and my sister had both gone to medical school in Italy. I started taking evening classes in Italian at the Italian Cultural Institute in Tel Aviv, and my father and sister helped me improve my language skills by speaking to me in Italian. On October of 1968, I began medical studies in Siena, Italy.

One day in 1970, in the midst of my studies in Siena, Italy, I felt uncharacteristically tired. I had a headache, and my energy was low. Instead of going to lectures, I took a rare day off and stayed at home in bed.

That afternoon, I heard a knock on my door. It was a state policeman, who told me to expect a phone call in the post office at four o'clock, from Yosef Even, my father-in-law. My brother-in-law, Chaim, having lived in Italy before, knew how to reach me through the local *questura* (police headquarters), and he must have told my father-in-law. I knew it had to be bad news.

I arrived early and sat anxiously in the post office, looking at the clock. Finally the call came. The noisy phone line was compounded by the shakiness in my father-in-law's voice. He told me that my father was gone, dead from a sudden heart attack.

My first reaction was pure shock. Then I thought about how I had felt all day. It was as if my body had been preparing me for the blow. The next thing I remember was running down the cobblestones of Via Banchi di Sopra towards Piazza Del Campo, the main public square in Siena, to get to the travel agency before they closed. The next morning, I was on the plane from Rome to Tel Aviv to attend the funeral.

In hindsight I think Monek was a role model for me in choosing geriatrics as my professional career. His concern for his patients and creative "thinking out of the box" in opening an onsite laboratory for testing poor elders with diabetes — people for whom access to the clinic was often difficult — has definitely informed the way I think about serving people. In 1986, I founded the Specialized Ambulatory Geriatric Assessment clinic (S+AGE) in Encino, California, where we emulated the "one-stop shop" approach for frail elders, simplifying things for them and their caregivers. During the recent COVID pandemic, I initiated an at-home visitation service using telehealth and in-person staff visits to homebound elderly, thus saving them the trouble of being driven to clinics. As I see Medicare in the USA and other health systems worldwide starting to recognize the public-health advantages of preventing illness over just treating it, it definitely resonates with me, reminding me of my father's initiatives in Ansbach.

Above all my father taught me that it is okay to dream, and to dream big. This gave me an outlet to build ideas and concepts that helped me personally and played a major role in my career. I adopted his proactive approach to problem-solving: his "go and get it" attitude, his drive and dedication to relieving human distress and suffering. I adopted, too, his person-centered approach in medicine: following the need, as opposed to following the money, and always looking how we can improve on what we do. These and other elements of my father's legacy have been pivotal in guiding and inspiring my own career in geriatrics.

CHAPTER 14

Beyond Survival

One of the warmest memories I have of my father is of a trip we took to Italy in May 1963, when I was in the eleventh grade. He was 60. We took a ship, the *Theodor Herzl*, to Genoa, Italy, the same port from which we first sailed to Israel in 1951, and from there we took the train to Milan. We spent a few weeks there with my sister Ewa, who was in medical school, studying for her finals. We went with her husband Chaim and her daughter Tamar to the Dolomites, where we hiked in those snowy mountains, and I heard yodeling for the first time.

From Milan, we got on the train again and traveled to the south of Italy, stopping in various places my father knew from his past. We spent time in Perugia, where he had gone to medical school, and Florence, where he and my mother had studied together. He still spoke fluent Italian, so it was very easy to get around. I remember a lot of sitting around tables in pensions or barber shops, my father chatting away with strangers and my having no idea what they were talking about.

I did sometimes notice his health challenges, especially when we were walking up some of those steep Italian hills. After coming to Israel, he had been diagnosed with diabetes. It was managed, but it is common for people with diabetes to develop cardiovascular ailments. He would frequently have to stop, out of breath, but never once did he suggest shortening the trip with me.

One day we entered a magnificent church in Florence and stared up at its soaring ceiling. After a few moments, my father murmured quietly to me, out of the corner of his mouth, "How does it make you feel?"

"Small" was all I could think of to say.

"Exactly," he agreed. "They build it big to make you feel small."

I have often thought about that exchange. I wonder if he was criticizing religion in general, or religious hypocrisy, or if he was remembering that day in Janowska when he decided there was no God. I can't ask him what he was thinking, and I'm not in a position to know whether my father was right about God or not. I do know, now, that he was a man who had survived the unimaginable and came out permanently scarred, but that his wounds did not stop him from spreading health and generosity and kindness.

That, to me, is the ultimate takeaway from the war. The survival and flourishing of my family and so many like them, despite all we have been through, is a testament to the potential of human beings to make the world better. The catastrophe they somehow managed to survive was the result of the actions of human beings, too — ordinary human beings like you and me.

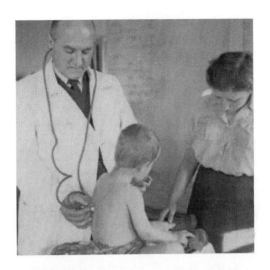

Figure 19: Dr. Kotarba (aka Osterweil), Children's House, Budapest

Figure 21: Children's House on Kövér Lajos Utsa 2, Budapest

Figure 22: From left: Avram, Hanka, Olga (Zahava), and Ushier

Figure 23: Dining room, Children's House, Budapest.

Figure 24: Ewa (blond, in center left) with Hungarian and Polish children, Budapest

Figure 25: Olga and Aron (first and second from left), Budapest

Figure 26: Children's home on Kövér Lajos Utsa 2, Budapest

*Figure 27: From right: Dr. Kotarba (Monek, first) and Hanka
(fourth) on a balcony of one of the safe houses in Budapest.*

Figure 28: Marisia (young woman in second row) and Ewa (third row, third from left) with Polish and Hungarian kids, Budapest

Figure 29: Fritsch (seated, center) with Monek (right), Ushier (left). Standing, from left: Ewa and Hela. Far right: Ewa's daughter, Tamar.

Figure 30: First row, from left: Ewa (sixth from left). Second row, from left: Hela (third); George Axelrod, (fifth, with cap); Marisia Offen (seventh), and other unidentified children, Jan Hus Memorial - Prague, 1945.

Figure 31: Little Marisia and her adoptive mother, Mrs. Klapholtz

Figure 32: Jerzyk's cousin, Ziuta Lamensdorf-Gutt

Figure 33: From left, Ziuta Lamensdorf-Gutt with Janka Tecko and Josef (Jerzyk), Warsaw, 1981

Figure 34: Ewa, Hela, and Josef (Jerzyk) in Strüth

Figure 35: Gusta Malinowski and Marisia Offen

Figure 36: Hela, Monek, and Ewa in Strüth

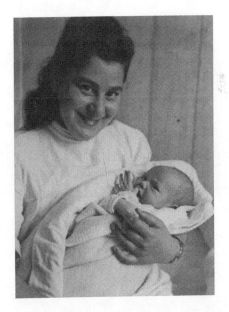

Figure 37: Marisia Offen holding the author

Figure 38: Osterweils and Ladners in Munich, circa 1949. Top row, from left: Marisia, Hela, Mila, Aron Osterweil, and Sylvia. Middle row, from left: Monek, Ewa, and Josef (Jerzyk). Bottom row, from left: author and Fredek Ladner.

Figure 39: Dr. Moshe (Monek) Osterweil, Medical Director, Bogenhousen Spital, Munich

Figure 40: Dr. Moshe (Monek) Osterweil, Gusta Malinowski,
Fritsch, Josef (Jerzyk), and Dr. Fuss, a dentist and family friend

Figure 41: Josef (Jerzyk), author, and Ewa, 1949

Figure 42: Josef (Jerzyk) and Ewa on the way to Children's Aid Society camp, October 1949

Figure 43: Julek Czoban and Jerzyk, Bleidorn, 1948

Figure 44: From left: Hospital administrator, Jerzyk with au pair Erika Marten, Monek holding the author, Hela, and Ewa, Munich, circa 1950

Figure 45: School at Bleidorn refugee camp. Hela, second standing from left. Ewa, seventh standing from left. Jerzyk in vest, bottom row, extreme right.

Figure 46: Opening Ceremony of MALBEN Hospital, Beer Yaakov, from left: seated 2nd Dr Pliskin, Standing Dr Moses (Monek) Osterweil(undated)

Aftermath

To a people that survived the Holocaust, every survivor, and their story, along with every descendant — every child, grandchild, and great-grandchild — is a victory. What happened to those I've named in these pages? Where are they now? And how does a family's story of those times come together?

I always knew about Monek's work as a doctor after the war, in Germany and in Israel: his generosity, his ingenuity, the impact he had on so many lives. On the day after my bar mitzvah, when he told me the story of seeing the children shot at Janowska, I got a glimpse into some of the more painful parts of his life. There were a few other moments, such as when Shlomo Arad came to visit us in Israel, and when Uncle Ushier brought Franz Fritsch to that birthday party, that I had a sense of what life had been like for my family during the war. It wasn't until after my father's death, however, that I learned how many lives he helped save, and how much he risked in doing so.

I learned about these events largely from my mother, without whom Monek couldn't have accomplished what he did, and who also risked her own life many times. The war had an enormous impact on my mother's life: time and again, she had to trust her intuition and exercise all her ingenuity to keep her and Ewa alive in perilous situations. My mother was a sensitive woman, much ruled by her feelings. She was observant and a good judge of character, with an undeniable clear-sighted practicality. She lived in a time when vocational opportunities for women were limited, but she made the most of her opportunities.

In addition to the work as a kindergarten teacher that she was originally trained for, she taught at many levels in a variety of settings, eventually being certified in Hebrew, History, Literature, Philosophy, and other subjects. She also always assisted my father in his work. After he died, she kept going, helping many more people, even singlehandedly running a breast cancer prevention clinic as a volunteer. She kept up a busy schedule of volunteer work until her late eighties. Even during her long years with increasing dementia, she remained a formidable presence, keeping all us on our toes. Once, when she was already quite demented, I observed her in one of her anxiety attacks, shaking and calling out to "Matko Boska," the Holy Mother. As I have related, she took Ewa to regular church services so they would pass as Catholics and had even bought her a colorful icon of Mother Mary at the church in Vác, an icon Ewa had found soothing. This leads me to believe the social-science research that faith and religious symbols may have a useful role for people in distress.

Hela passed away in 2009, just three months short of her 100th birthday. Though she had often played a supporting role while Monek was alive, after he died she was better able to face the past. She became my storyteller, starting in 1987 on our trip to London, with me taking copious notes. Credit for the process I have embarked on belongs largely to her. I have added more chapters to this compilation on every visit to Israel since, trying to document my family's war experiences.

Ewa married Haim Zakut, and both had successful careers in medicine. Ewa, now Dr. Havah Zakut, practiced family medicine. She cared for many families of new immigrants to Israel, ran innovative clinics inspired by the one-stop clinic Monek opened, and improved communication with specialists to make her patients more comfortable. She received an award from the health system CEO for excellence in her work with Ethiopian immigrants in Israel. She retired after a long tenure at the Kupat Cholim Klalit and is devoting her time to painting and spending time with her children and grandchildren. Her husband, Haim, had an interesting career, first as a researcher at the Weizmann Institute of Science, then as a specialist in reproductive medicine and gynecology and as a faculty member at Tel Aviv University's Sackler Medical School. Ewa and Haim have two daughters, Tamar and Tali, and two sons, Yaron and Eran, with a total of nine grandchildren, who live in Israel and the United States.

Ewa, who adored both my parents, felt a huge sense of loss after our father's death but did not express much to me about her feelings at the time. During our mother's long decline with dementia, however, Ewa opened up about her experiences from the remote and more recent past. Watching our mother sinking into a demented state — slowly losing the person who had saved and protected her during the difficult days in the ghetto, the deportations, the journeys, the hiding places, and who brought her to safety, alone — was difficult for Ewa to endure. My only regret during that period is that, living on another continent, I did not spend enough time with Ewa, listening and empathizing — that for years I was too focused on trying to fix problems associated with our mother's decline, rather than attending to the people around her, like Ewa and my niece, Tamar, who shouldered the main burden of overseeing my mother's care. I regret very much this lack of awareness and sensitivity to their pain and stress. I hope and believe that I have learned from this experience and have become a better person since then.

My cousin Jerzyk — now Josef — moved to the United States in the early 1960s after graduating from the Technion in Haifa and distinguished service in the IDF as an engineer. He obtained advance degrees, holds a list of patents, and made significant contributions to Israel's security and to the field of telecommunications. He is now retired after a distinguished career in electrical engineering. We speak on the phone several times a week, discussing various topics and common interests. For example, I recruited him to solve various geriatric medical problems, a collaboration that led to several inventions and registered patents. He has a daughter, Yael; a son, Zvi; and six grandchildren. Today he is happily married to Mary Ann Winter, his second wife, who brought him the gift of four more grandchildren and one great-granddaughter. Jerzyk contributed to the financial support of Joanna (Janka) Tecko, who protected him in Warsaw, until the end of her life, also giving testimony at Yad Vashem for her to be declared a Righteous Among the Nations.

Like Ewa, Josef's opening up was an iterative process. During all the years he and I shared a bedroom in my parents' home, he was tight-lipped about his wartime experiences. The first time the story of what happened in Warsaw came up was in 1987, on one of Josef's frequent business trips to Los Angeles. He came the day after my wife, Erna, learned of her father's death in Israel, very shortly after she returned from visiting him. Since she could not leave again for the funeral, she was sitting shiva in our house. Trying to be supportive, Josef said, "I know it is sad, losing your father. At least you will know where he is buried." He himself does not, as he related to us. Later, on his seventieth birthday, I forced him to share his story with his kids; I still choke up whenever I tell it. In the process of exchanging details about my writing, he realized that this is his story as well.

Despite the happy and productive sides of his life, Josef has retained a good deal of trauma and lasting pain, like so many who endured the events of the Holocaust. In later years, for example, he has become increasingly haunted by feelings of guilt and anguish towards his parents. He feels guilty for not picking up on the warning signs when the robbers prevented him, the week earlier, from visiting his father. "I should have known. I should have warned him. If I had, he might not have been killed." He also feels a lot of anguish that his parents did not see the writing on the wall, continuing their comfortable life in Tarnów instead of leaving Poland and joining their friends in Palestine while there was still time. Finally, he is haunted by the question of why they did not take the opportunity to escape with Ushier and Fritsch. Maybe his mother, Faiga, did not want to leave her father in the ghetto. Maybe they were just afraid to take a chance. He'll never know.

Uncle Aron Osterweil was sent to Siberia with Uncle Fredek Ladner and his nephew, Ruzia's son David. All three survived. Aron made it to a house run by "Dr. Kotarba" in Budapest. He married another survivor that he met at my father's house: Mila, my favorite aunt. They lived briefly in Schwarzbach, Germany, where Aron ran a successful women's-apparel business before making aliya to Israel in 1949, a year after the State was declared. Aron and Mila had a son, my beloved cousin Yossi, with whom I shared many fun times during my childhood. Yossi retired after a distinguished career as chief of the Haifa power plant for the Israel Electric Corporation, Israel's national electricity authority. He is married and has two children, a daughter and a son.

David Ladner's father, Herman Ladner, remained in the United States, where he remarried and helped bring David to the US. David married Annette Gralnick and had three children — Mark, Susan, and Fred — and six grandchildren. David's children contributed a document he wrote that sheds more details about his odyssey, which I've included here as an appendix, below.

Uncle Ushier Osterweil and his wife Hanka, as I have related, ended up in Tel Aviv with their son, Avram, and daughter Olga. Ushier and Hanka passed away many years ago. My cousin Avram Osterweil married and lives in Israel, where he became a successful businessman. We stay in touch occasionally. He has a daughter, Shelly, who lives in the U.S, a son, and two grandchildren, who live in Israel. His sister, Olga, took the Hebrew name Zehava and became an accomplished educational psychologist and faculty member at the Hebrew University in Jerusalem. She had a brief marriage with no children, and, sadly, died rather young from cancer.

Sala Ladner was a member of Hashomer Hatzair and also emigrated to Palestine, probably in the late 1920s, where she married Zvi Idelson. They had three children — Dan, Micha, and Yael — and eleven grandchildren.

Fredek Ladner left Tarnów around 1920, probably to avoid the Polish military draft, and went to Lüdenscheid, Germany, where he married Herta, a nurse, and set up a crate-manufacturing business. He and Herta remained there until 1938 when they, along with all Polish Jewish residents, were expelled by the Nazis. They returned to Poland and lived in Kraków and Tarnów, while Fredek escaped to Russia and later was deported to Siberia with his nephew, Ruzia Ladner's son David, and with my father's brother Aron. All three survived. Fredek was ultimately reunited with the family in Bleidorn, where he brightened the life of us kids with gifts.

Fredek spent a short time in Sweden, where he worked as busboy cleaning dishes in a restaurant. He told me that he gained a lot of weight there: the Swedes came to the restaurant mainly to consume alcohol; this required them to buy a meal, which they seldom touched. After his experiences in Russia, Fredek felt bad throwing all this great food away, so he helped himself. From Sweden he went to Germany, where he reunited with old friends. Later he met and married an American woman named Lillian and emigrated to the United States. The marriage ended in a divorce, but they had one son, Leon, who lives in the U.S. In the late 1960s, Fredek moved to Israel. He died in his nineties while having his weekly *shvitz* (steam bath), his favorite pastime.

Oskar Ladner was an engineer who worked in Russia and Germany before emigrating in the 1930s to Palestine with his wife, Renia. They did not have children. Oskar worked until his last day for the Israel Electric Corporation.

Little Marisia married a forest ranger from Yugoslavia and lives with her husband and their daughters in Israel.

Marisia Offen, the girl whom my aunt Hanka had met in the Tarnów community center and brought to Budapest, lived in Israel as Miriam Steinlauf. She became part of our family and was very close to my father: they worked together in Munich and later at the Be'er Yaakov Hospital, where she served as a head pediatric nurse. She married Avram Steinlauf, who died a few years ago, in his nineties. They had two sons, three granddaughters, and one great-granddaughter. One of their sons, Dr. Shmuel Steinlauf, is a retired officer in Israel's medical corps, a physician, and chief of an internal medicine unit at Sheba, one of Israel's top hospitals. Marisia passed away on February 7, 2022. She was 93 years old.

George Axelrod came to live in one of the protected houses that my father ran. He managed to recuperate fully and to adjust well to orphanage life. His parents later found each other and then him, but when they learned how close George had grown to the group of children and to my father, they realized that it was best to let him stay there for a while. He eventually rejoined his parents in Strüth, Germany, then obtained a visa and made his permanent home in the United States, where he studied chemical engineering and taught at a New York college. He married and had two daughters, one of whom became teacher, the other an attorney.

Now that I know so much more about what these family members and friends went through, I am amazed that they all not only survived but so thoroughly thrived.

Like so many other families, ours had its share not only of survivors but of victims as well, not to be forgotten.

Of my father's other siblings, as I have related here, my uncle Herman Osterweil was shot to death. His wife, Faiga, was rounded up in Tarnów ghetto and presumably killed, leaving their son, my cousin Jerzyk, as the only survivor of their line.

The fate of Monek's only sister, Ruzia, is unknown; no one spoke of her.

Of my mother's siblings, Ruzia Ladner married a cousin, Herman Ladner, and had three sons. Ruzia disappeared with their son Fredek. Another son, Henek, was taken to a labor camp. Their son David was the only survivor among his siblings.

Rena Ladner married and divorced. Her only son, Adam, disappeared. Both are presumed dead.

My Uncle Fredek Ladner's wife, Herta, died in Belzec.

We do not know where my mother's brother Herman Ladner was when the Germans invaded Poland. He disappeared, with no eye witnesses who could corroborate his wherabouts. Ruzia, her sons Fredek and Henek, and my mother's brother Herman are all presumed dead.

The increasingly few survivors that are left, along with many of my generation, the children of survivors, often urge the younger generations: Never forget! I hope our children will look back at the Holocaust as a stark lesson on what human beings are capable of, a lesson we hope never to repeat. We must remember the past in order not to repeat its mistakes.

Looking back on the period, however, it is too easy to remember the victims *only* as victims, and to waste energy hating the Nazi perpetrators. We should remember the people: their lives, their accomplishments. And, if my father's legacy taught me anything, we should leave hate out of it. Instead, we should look forward, and set our hands to do whatever we can to repair this troubled world.

Appendix: David Ladner's War Experience
By David Ladner[9]

When war broke out on September 1, 1939, I was at home, having returned from the compulsory P.W. (Polish ROTC) camp. I remember watching on September 3, from the turret of the house on Krakowska Street, as German airplanes bombed in the vicinity of Tarnów. Earlier, on August 28, 1939, German saboteurs had blown up part of the Tarnów railroad station. Twenty people were killed. Perhaps because of this action, students, members of the P.W., were called up for guard duty. My first duty was near that railroad station, where I smoked my first cigarette. I also saw my first war victim, a dismembered horse. This sight has remained with me forever.

On September 4, realizing that the German armies were nearing the city, I volunteered, along with some of my friends, to join a P.W. unit being formed then. The volunteers were issued old rifles with no ammunition. The ammunition, with other supplies, including the unit's money, accompanied the unit on separate horse-drawn wagons. The unit was marching east, presumably to join the regrouping regular army.

---

9   The author of this account is the son of Hela Osterweil's eldest sister, Ruzia, who married a cousin named Herman Ladner.

On the morning following our departure, the unit found itself without its commanding officer and without its supplies. They had disappeared during the night. I kept on marching east, my feet bleeding from my father's boots, which were too big for me. The march was not a peaceful one. The roads, clogged with retreating soldiers and civilian refugees, kept being bombed and machine gunned by German planes. (Years later, it became known that this was part of the German blitzkrieg plan to cause panic on the roads.) The planes flew so low that it was possible to see the pilots.

On the road, I met up with my schoolmate from Safah Berurah,[10] Dalek Spielman (Adler), who was riding in the same direction with his uncle on a horse-drawn wagon. They took me along, but shortly thereafter, they were robbed of the horses, the wagon, and everything on it by an armed Ukrainian band. Since the German Army was motorized and the Spielmans and I were marching on foot, we were overtaken and captured by the Germans. By that time I was no longer carrying a rifle, and my uniform was still a P.W. uniform, not a standard army uniform. After a few hours I was released, but not before receiving a kick in the behind from a Nazi soldier upon answering in the affirmative the question, "Are you a Jew?" I cannot recall what happened to the Spielmans.

I decided to return home but was prohibited from doing that by the Germans, so I kept walking east. I found myself in a Jewish shtetl, probably Bełżec, where I was well received by the Chasidim and their *rebbe*. It was the first shtetl that I had ever seen. The center of the town had little wooden houses. There were stores, with people living on the upper stories. There was a wooden synagogue in the

---

10 Safah Berurah ("clear language") was a society for the propagation of the Hebrew language.

center of the shtetl. I was fed and given lodging in one of the houses, as were other refugees walking along the roads. I think that it may have been the eve of Rosh Hashonah.[11] The following morning the Germans arranged for a pogrom. They burned the Jewish communal buildings in the center of the town and forced the Jews with beating and kicking to the river, where they were made to haul buckets of water to put out the fires. It was great fun for the soldiers and the Ukrainian peasants brought in from surrounding villages. There was a lot of robbing and looting.

I joined a crowd of the Polish and Ukrainian onlookers. I was feverish from a bad cold, and I did not realize the full horror of what was going on. As things turned out, I was spared. Perhaps I was saved by my looks (I did not look Jewish) and the peasant-type coat that I was wearing, which had been given to me by Mr. Spielman. When things quieted down, I resumed marching east. My next stop was a larger town, also predominantly Jewish, Rawa Ruska, where I became really sick and was given hospitality by a Jewish family. Germans were in the town, but there were no persecutions yet. Coincidental with my recovery, the Soviet army marched into Rawa Ruska, according to a previous agreement with the German government. The Jewish population was jubilant, especially so because the first Red Army officers who rode into town spoke Yiddish.

Shortly thereafter, my uncle, Dr. Monek Osterweil, found me and brought me to Lwów, which had been occupied by the Soviets on September 22. In Lwów, I was prevailed upon to enter school, probably by the urging of relatives and from letters from my mother. The school I entered had once been a Jewish gymnasium similar to the

---

11 Rosh Hashonah, the Jewish New Year, began in the evening of September 13, 1939.

one I had attended in Tarnów. However, under the Soviets, the language of instruction was not Polish but Yiddish. Soon Yiddish was changed to Ukrainian. Since I was unfamiliar with either language I, like the rest of the students, had great difficulty studying. It was very strange having mathematics and chemistry taught in Yiddish.

A greater difficulty yet was caused by lack of any means of support. I was provided with a bed in the apartment of a Jewish family of modest means. The head of the family was an insurance agent. They were very nice to me, especially their daughter, who was about my age. Of course they had to be paid for the lodging. I received some money from Monek Osterweil and some from another uncle, Herman Ladner. Soon, my mother managed to send me, through smugglers, items that I could wear or sell on the black market. On the black market, I also tried to sell liquor in order to earn some money. The liquor was provided to me and to my schoolmate, Haskel Kurtz (from Tarnów) by the aunt of another former schoolmate. She was the manager of her own distillery, which had been nationalized by the Soviets, and was selling the liquor to us at prices set by the government. I remember standing on the corner with my friend in the cold weather, not knowing how to sell our wares. Occasionally there were police raids, and we lost whatever we had.

(In 1966 or 1967, while living in Queens, N.Y., my wife Annette got a phone call from Haskel Kurz, who was on a business trip in the USA, inquiring whether Dudek Ladner lived at this address. He had heard that I was alive and in New York. He called all the Ladners in the New York City phone book and finally reached me. In 1969, our entire family visited with Haskel Kurz and his family in Haifa, and we are still in touch with his widow and daughter. Haskel died of cancer a few years after this reunion.)

Under such dire circumstances, often being without food or funds, I was often absent from classes and was very poorly nourished. However I managed to graduate from the Jewish gymnasium on June 26, 1940.

Homesick and desperate, I, like thousands of others, registered with the German commission in Lwów to return home. The return home never happened for anybody, but all those who had registered, like many others considered undesirable, were rounded up and sent to the Gulag. Thanks to Aron Osterweil's foresight, the three of us, my Uncle Fredek Ladner, my uncle Monek's brother Aron Osterweil, and I were awaiting the roundup in one apartment. Thus we were considered a family by the political police, since I was a minor. This ruse spared Fredek and Aron from being sent to a forced labor camp. Instead, all of us were deported to a work settlement in the far north of Russia. I remember trying to convince the officer who was interviewing me that, as a graduate of a Soviet high school, I should be sent somewhere where I could continue my education. The officer assured me that this would certainly be the case. This was probably early July 1940. (Letters to my father from me and from the Druckers, family friends, clarify some dates.)

We were taken on trucks, escorted by soldiers with rifles with bayonets to a railroad siding. The long train stayed there long enough for relatives and friends from Lwów to say goodbye to the deportees. I was visited by two friends, Ada Drucker and Miss Schweitzer, the daughter of the family I had been staying with. I think they brought me candy for the journey.

We had a harrowing journey, in closed cattle cars, guarded by armed guards with dogs, allowed out of the cars only occasionally to relieve ourselves under the trains. Despite being guarded, Aron managed to slip out of the train while the train was stopped for a long time somewhere around Kiev. He managed to get to Kiev, bought some candy and, not knowing where else to go without any documents, bought a ticket, took a passenger train, and caught up with the transport a few days later. The journey lasted for days until, hungry and thirsty, we arrived at a large railroad transfer point for the Gulag, Kotlas.

In Kotlas, we, along with other prisoners, were loaded onto a boat, which proceeded north on the Pinega River. The voyage ended in a small town, a regional center, Verkhnyaya Toyma. A guarded convoy awaited us there. The convoy consisted of mobilized peasants from the area with horse-drawn wagons from collective farms. Our possessions were loaded onto the wagons and we, the deportees, had to walk alongside. The driver of the wagon with our possessions was a fellow my age who surprised me by being able to recite long passages of Pushkin poems. (Years later I suspected him of being not a peasant boy but an agent of the NKVD, the secret police.)

After a long march, the convoy arrived in a work settlement in the midst of the taiga, the primeval evergreen forest. (From letters it seems that we reached Pyshma on July 26, 1940.) I was in no mood at that time to appreciate the surroundings, but months later, in the wintertime, I would sometimes, during work breaks, walk off into the woods to just admire the landscape.

The settlement was called Pyshma-Edama. It was situated near the Pinega River, a tributary of the Northern Dvina River. Such settlements had been organized in the 1920s or '30s for the then-deported "kulaks,"[12] who constructed the buildings after having been

---

12 *Kulaks* were land-owning peasants, who were vilified during the Russian Revolution as enemies of the poorer class of peasants. Under Stalin, the kulaks' land was confiscated, and they were deported to labor colonies or executed.

deposited in the midst of the woods. Many died during the process. The settlement consisted of a group of long log cabins, which were to serve as the living quarters for the deportees — men, women, and children. There were also a few communal buildings, like a Russian bath, kitchen, dining hall, and, most important, the quarters of the NKVD officer, the settlement commandant and its only armed overseer. The other overseer represented the state-owned timber company, whose employees the deportees became.

Our welcome consisted of a statement by the commandant to the effect that we would never leave there. He also added a Russian saying, "*Privikat' nada! Kak ne priviknesh tak zdokhnesh.*" This meant that we had to get used to everything. If we didn't, we'd perish — the Russian word for *perish* was the one used only for animals.

Water was drawn from deep wells; there were no indoor toilet facilities, no sewers. The local newspaper was cut up and used for toilet paper. In winter snow and ice were melted and collected to use for laundry. Cigarettes were made by rolling newspaper for wrappers and using crushed birch leaves or makhorka, a coarse tobacco. I was glad that I had learned to smoke because work breaks were called for smoking. Smoking was especially important in the summertime as a protection from the giant mosquitoes.

From early morning until dusk, people were marched out deep into the woods to fell trees. They were trained in this occupation, which was new to them, by a local old man, who was also given the task of sharpening the handsaws and axes.

The workers were paid on a piecework basis. Needless to say, they were unable to fulfill their work quota, and their pay was insufficient to pay for their upkeep. This was especially so since ten percent of their earned money went to the NKVD "for taking care of us." Bread was brought in twice a week; the bread ration was

750 grams per person, per day. Women were primarily employed at light labor — cooking, doing laundry, cleaning, chopping firewood — and received smaller bread rations. In winter, "light labor" included keeping the ice railroad clear. The ice railroad was built at the onset of the winter frosts by pouring water over the snow to enable the horse-driven heavy sleds to transport the felled trees to the river shore.

In addition to the bread ration, there was flour soup, with an occasional scrap of meat. There was also hot water. When they were available, which was not often, one could also buy cheap candy, Russian cigarettes, and some other items in the canteen. The complete lack of fresh fruit and vegetables caused a constant threat of avitaminosis,[13] such as scurvy. To prevent such diseases, the kitchen occasionally received quantities of dried onions. All the supplies, including bread, were brought in by horse and wagons or sleds in winter from the port of Verkhnyaya Toyma. Our original journey from that port to Pyshma had been a walk of four days' duration. Since we were not allowed to leave, we did not know how close the nearest settlement was.

Sometime after their arrival, people started receiving food parcels from relatives. We could not have survived without them. Fredek, Aron, and I received food packages from Herman Ladner (Fredek's and Rozia's brother) and from Lusiek Offner, a cousin, who was managing a travelling troupe of performers. Rozia, my mother, tried to send packages through Uncle Herman Ladner while he was in Lwów. I also received clothing packages from my father in the United States, though I cannot remember whether that were during this period or later on. The clothing packages had labels with red

---

13 A group of diseases brought on by vitamin deficiency.

stars on them, which was surprising: red stars were the emblem of the Soviet Union, but these were from Macy's in New York, whose logo was a red star.

Medical care was provided by sporadic visits from a "feltsher," a medical assistant who had two remedies for all illnesses: one was an aspirin, the second a diuretic. At least once that I remember, an older man with high fever was taken by sled to a distant hospital, where he subsequently died. There was also at least one case of a terminal heart attack. Once a week, after work, there was a visit to the Russian bathhouse, a log cabin with a pile of rocks, heated by a fire, on which water was poured to create steam. In the wintertime the water for washing ourselves came from melted snow. During the week the bathhouse was used by the women for the laundering of clothes. Soap was usually available for sale in the little store, as was tooth powder.

The real trials came in winter, which arrives early in that region. The workers were sold winter clothing: cotton-filled pants, short coats (known as *fufaykas*), and felt boots. They still froze, especially early in the morning. At lunch they would make bonfires to warm themselves while eating flour soup brought in from the settlement. Work in the woods ceased when the temperature fell below minus 60 C.

I was exempted from heavy work until my 18th birthday. (January 23, 1941). After that I, too, was felling giant trees using a hand saw and an axe. Having grown up in an urban setting and a very protected environment, I had never seen a saw or an axe, much less used them. Most of the deportees had not been accustomed to physical labor, except, perhaps, for Uncle Fredek. They were primarily business people. Needless to say, this labor was very hard for me. I developed a backache, which would not leave me for years. I was "diagnosed" as having kidney troubles and given some unknown powder for it. It did not help.

Since I was the only deportee who knew Russian, I was assigned the job of keeping account of the cut lumber and of classifying it according to quality and type of tree. I had seen this done at my father's sawmill, and I exaggerated my qualifications. The classification was done by stamping the back of the tree trunk with a special hammer. I also served as an informal representative to the two overseers. In the process of performing these "duties," I was once hit and threatened with a revolver by the commandant, after I had complained to him that the work quota was too high and the bread ration too low.

The other seasons had their own trials. The felling of trees ceased with the advent of spring. The lumber had been stacked at the river shore, preparatory to being floated down to Northern Dvina and from there to the port of Archangel or Arkhangelsk. Uncle Fredek volunteered for the very dangerous job of logrolling, that is, standing on top of the bundle of floating logs and controlling their movement with long pikes. He was very good at this job, earning compliments and higher pay from the supervisors.

The short summer brought swarms of giant mosquitoes, which were especially tormenting to the workers cutting hay in bogs. Some people became ill with malaria. But summer had its rewards too. There was no fresh fruit available in the settlement. But in summer, in their free time, people would go to the woods to collect lingonberries, a good source of vitamin C.

In winter, the barracks were heated by wood-burning stoves. There was no lighting, and I wrote my letters by the light of burning birch bark. We slept on wooden pallets, covered with whatever we could find. The dormitories housed families: men, women, and children.

We were cut off from news. The only information available was that from the official Soviet sources, bragging of German advances on the Western front and of the Soviet-Nazi alliance. For obvious reasons the few letters received were confined to "safe" information. The situation changed somewhat with the outbreak of the Soviet-German war. The news reaching us then started mentioning some of the German atrocities in the Nazi-occupied territories and of the activities of the Polish government-in-exile, which had previously been considered an enemy. We, of course, had no idea of the real situation within the Soviet Union. The government propaganda, on radio and in newspapers, was the only source of news to anybody in the Soviet Union. The news from the front after the German invasion of the Soviet Union began on June 22, 1941, was of constant victories of the Red Army, diametrically opposite to the real situation.

Sometime after the invasion began, the Polish government in London succeeded in obtaining an amnesty agreement from Moscow. Under this agreement, all Polish citizens incarcerated or deported by the Soviets were to be freed. The information was late in getting to Pyshma-Edama. Even when the instructions reached there, there were efforts made to convince the deportees to remain there as "free workers," with higher pay and no police supervision.

Thus, it wasn't until late summer of 1941 that I, together with Uncle Fredek and with Aron Osterweil, who had joined us after being freed from the forced labor camp, were allowed to leave. Those who decided to leave, which included almost all the deportees in the camp, were shown a map of the Soviet Union and told to choose their destination. We were barred from going to any large cities or near any borders. My relatives and I decided to go south to Central Asia, where we knew it would be warmer. Central Asia was thousands of miles from where we were. No transportation was provided, and no money was given to us. We were given ID papers showing that we were free to travel. (In the Soviet Union all people were supposed to stay in the locality where they lived and worked. Travel was only by special permission and was usually only on work assignment.)

We had to retrace the route we had taken to Pyshma. That meant a walk of many miles to Verkhnyaya Toyma, the port on the river Pinega, from which we would take a boat to Kotlas, the nearest railroad station. Time was of the essence since the rainy season was approaching, which would render the roads impassable. It was not an easy march. I was suffering from boils on my legs, a result of my work in submerged bogs. I was also undernourished and weak. For long stretches of the road, my Uncle Fredek carried me on his shoulders. We obtained food and lodging on the road through the hospitality of the peasants in the villages we were passing through.

On our arrival in Verkhnyaya Toyma we found work at the port loading and unloading boats. My Uncle Fredek excelled at this work, but I at first had great difficulty in carrying the heavy sacks of flour and sugar and heaving them high up to be stacked. When we had earned enough money for our passage, we boarded a ship for Kotlas. In Kotlas we had to register with the police to be allowed to travel farther. Then we had to wait for available places on the train going south. The wait was a long one, as there were thousands of released prisoners trying to go south and elsewhere. The railroad line from Kotlas was the only connection to all the Russian railroads.

The railroad trip south to our planned destination was accomplished in stages, from one large railroad station to another. The war was on, and the many military trains had priority over passenger ones. There were also numerous trains filled with evacuees from Russian cities fleeing from the fast-moving German armies. These too had priority. Freight trains loaded with entire evacuated factories were moving east to the Ural Mountains. All this movement caused me and my companions to wait at overcrowded stations, often for days at a time. Cold and hunger were a problem. We had no food and no money to buy food with. We usually travelled on freight trains or on passenger trains, on the platforms between the cars, since we had no tickets. I still remember once sharing space on the platform between the cars with a frozen corpse. I also remember begging for food from the evacuees, not always successfully. They, the members of the urban elites (others were not evacuated), looked down on us, emaciated, bedraggled and obviously former prisoners. Once, I recall, somewhere in the Urals, that I succeeded in getting potato peels from a family roasting potatoes at a fire near the railroad. Often, I would be separated from my uncle and from Aron, as all of us couldn't usually board the same train. In Sverdlovsk (now Yekaterinburg) I was treated for nearly-frozen toes in a hostel for evacuees.

From Sverdlovsk, still trying to travel south, we went through Chelyabinsk, then west through Zlatoust to Ufa, the capital of the Bashkir Autonomous Republic (now Bashkortostan). This being a capital, we were not allowed to remain there. We went to a *kolkhoz* or collective farm nearby, where we worked. We mainly did farm work. I remember helping with threshing wheat and being covered with dust from head to foot. I also remember driving an oxcart in a caravan to an oil refinery in Sterlitamak to get diesel oil for the farm's machinery. We worked for food only; for extra money we hired ourselves out to the members of the kolkhoz for sawing and chopping firewood. Aron was the one who would get the jobs, and Uncle Fredek and I did the actual work. The proceeds were shared with Aron, who was the entrepreneur, always wearing his fur coat. He was always resourceful.

The Bashkirs, a Moslem people, were very nice to us. The kolkhoz management assigned us to quarters with different families. My host family consisted of a couple with two children. They all lived in one room with a raised platform serving as a dining table and as a sleeping area. I shared this arrangement with them and shared their main meal, which consisted of soup with some dumplings and scraps of horsemeat. I also served as their interpreter on occasion, as they knew no Russian, and the government officials visiting the farm did not know Bashkir. After a while I had learned quite a few words in Bashkir, which is a Turkic language. At one time I manned the local Military Commission station to answer the telephone in Russian. This was one of the two telephones in the village. It was certainly strange to have a foreigner, recently released from detention, performing this duty. The local young men, having had some schooling, would have known Russian, but they had been drafted to the army. There were almost no young men around, and I remember being popular with the local girls.

With the coming of spring 1942, hunger arrived at the village. The supply of grains was exhausted. The government requisitioned even the seed grain. The catastrophic situation turned into a disaster when it was discovered that the spring crop of wheat had been hit by a fungus, making the grain inedible. It was time for Aron and Fredek and me to move on.

Still intent on getting to Central Asia, we went south to a large industrial city of Chkalov (now Orenburg) in the Southern Urals, the gateway to Central Asia. Getting food in the city was a problem for us, since we lacked formal jobs and the ration cards that would go with them. We decided to try our luck in a farming area. The nearest agricultural center was Ilek, some 70 miles southwest, and that is where we went, hitching rides on trucks. There we were assigned by the police (with whom we had to register each time we got to a new place) to work in different farms in the region. We lost touch with each other for a while.

My kolkhoz had me employed as an assistant on a tractor pulling a plow. My job, sitting on a seat attached to the plow, was to lift the plow up or down depending on the contour of the soil. The job was unbelievably dirty, and I was glad when sometime later I was promoted. This new job consisted of measuring the plowed fields using a primitive measuring rod and keeping account of the work done and the fuel expended. The results were disastrous. The fields were enormous, and I got hopelessly lost in my measurements. On top of this, the foreman of the tractor brigade was stealing fuel. Thus, the fuel usage and the area plowed did not add up. Since I was responsible for the accounting, I was hauled before a court and threatened with arrest. Soon it became apparent that I was no worse than a dupe in this affair. I was, however, expelled from the kolkhoz and went back to the town of Ilek.

Ilek was a little old town with picturesque wooden buildings in the center and some newer brick houses around it. After my arrival, I was dependent on odd jobs for my survival. Manpower being short at that time, it was usually possible to get food by working for residents of the town. There were long periods of hunger, however, and it was not easy to find a place to stay. Once, I got quarters at a house of the Regional First Secretary of the Communist Party, the highest official in town. This must have been after I received a package from my father, which I promptly sold in the bazaar. The proceeds enabled me to pay rent to the official's wife, whose husband was at the front. The woman's mother was very good to me. She was a religious person, Russian Orthodox, and she saw taking care of former prisoners as her duty. The landlady herself, while cool to somebody who had been previously repressed as a political "element," still allowed me to use her husband's library. This was the first and last time since I had left Lwów that I had access to books. It wasn't until years later that I found out how lucky I had been. Among the books in the library were some proscribed works, which had not been available to readers in the Soviet Union since the late twenties, including some Dostoevsky novels and even some Soviet-era writers. I had to change quarters periodically. My shaky position in town, as a released prisoner and a foreigner to boot, made it difficult for the various landlords to rent space to me. The space usually consisted of a cot in some corner.

I was renting space in the cellar of a substantial house belonging to the head of the local police when I caused embarrassment to my landlord. Sometime in the summer of 1942, during a campaign of forcing Poles to accept Soviet citizenship, a political police officer came to the house. He kept insisting that I accept Soviet citizenship. I kept refusing, saying that I was born in Poland and saw no need to change my citizenship. I was afraid that doing so would prevent my returning home after the war. The head of the police, my landlord, was told to arrest me and put me in the county jail. I spent several days in a cell with itinerant Gypsies and was repeatedly threatened during interrogations, the political policeman's (NKVD) revolver placed prominently on the desk. They could shoot me like a dog, they pointed out. No one would even know.

I was forced to yield. I finally accepted the Soviet passport, with my nationality shown as "Jewish." Naturally, I had to move again. I moved many times while in Ilek.

While working in a kolkhoz, I recall being assigned to help in driving a herd of swine to a far-away military base. The trip, on foot, for the pigs and their escorts took a number of days. While the men had some provisions, the pigs had to subsist on whatever food they could forage on the way. Needless to say, not all of the pigs arrived at their destination and those that did were pretty skinny. Nevertheless, the officers at the base, housed in earthen bunkers, were overjoyed with the transport of fresh meat for the officers' kitchen. They repaid the escorts with meals and food for their return march to the kolkhoz.

One's feet were not the only means of locomotion in Ilek. The transporting of goods was also done with the help of draft animals. Most of the horses had been taken by the army, but oxen and even camels, both long haired and double-humped, were used. In the wintertime a camel would pull a loaded sled, with the driver kneeling in the front of the sled. They were not speedy animals and I still remember how cold I was while driving them. They could also be pretty nasty, baring their big yellow teeth and spitting occasionally in the driver's face. The oxen, while more placid, presented other problems. They were stubborn, and it was difficult to convince them to move at a reasonable pace and to get them to follow directions. Once, at least, the ox pulling a sled loaded with brush for the Russian oven knew his way better than I, his driver. The ox insisted on going his way, which turned out to be the right way.

Once, I shared a room with a family of evacuees from Moscow. We all slept on the floor, mother, daughter and I. The father was in a forced labor camp at the time: he had been arrested, together with other editors of the *Great Soviet Encyclopedia*, for "political errors." His wife had to renounce him to escape persecution. Toward the end of the war the family was reunited in Moscow, but the released prisoner died shortly thereafter of a heart attack. The daughter, Rima Davidovna Geller, was seventeen, a graduate of a good Moscow high school, and I finally had someone I could talk to. I can remember sitting with her on a bazaar table, early on a wintry Sunday morning, teaching her to sing "Hatikva."[14] Rima's mother knew Hebrew but was afraid to use it, since its use was prohibited by the Soviets as a "nationalist deviation." (Yiddish was permitted.) I maintained a correspondence with Rima until I left the Soviet Union.

At another time, a refugee mother from Kiev wanted me to marry her daughter, once promising me a cow and at another time promising to arrange entrance to the well-known Kazan medical school and to support me during my studies. All I could think of then was going home to my family.

I was worried about my family in Tarnów. The year was 1943 and both by reading between the lines of the official war reports and by rumors floating around it became clear that horrible things were happening under the German occupation. Two years had passed since the last receipt of mail from my mother, after the outbreak of war between Germany and the Soviet Union on June 21, 1941. After the Soviet Army's victory at Stalingrad I tried to enlist in the Soviet Army but was rejected under the false pretense of myopia. (This was the time when the Soviets were drafting the "blind and the lame.") Sometime after this, however, I was called up to fill a quota of local draftees for the Labor Battalions. Knowing that this was a direct path to death, as such units were made up of the "untrustworthy" soldiers, who were sent into minefields and other extremely dangerous places, I decided to run away. The group of those draftees was being led under armed guard to a collection point that was a few days' march away. One night when everyone was asleep, I succeeded in escaping.

---

14 "Hatikva" (The Hope) was written by the Polish-Jewish poet Naftali Herz Imber. An edited version became the anthem of the Zionist movement and later of the State of Israel.

Naturally, I could not return to Ilek. My documents had been left with the guard of the convoy. I made my way to the big city of Chkalov, where I hoped to fade into the crowd. I stayed in Chkalov until the repatriation in 1946.

Finding work was not difficult. After spending a couple of nights in the railroad station, among hundreds of other homeless people, I managed to get to the nearest factory, which happened to be producing machine tools used to manufacture arms. They were glad to hire anyone who walked in. My lack of identification papers was somehow taken care of by the personnel department, which as usual in the Soviet Union was connected to the NKVD. I was assigned to do unskilled labor. The pay was so small as to be almost nonexistent, but I was given ration cards for bread and for whatever other food was available in the government stores. None of this was sufficient for one to live on. Sometimes food supplies were distributed by the factory. Once, on the eve of Yom Kippur, Comrade Wilkins, one of the factory managers, a Jew, gave out white bread and vodka to the Jewish workers. We did not know whether this was out of ignorance or chicanery.

After work I would try to find odd jobs. The best such job was at one of the local flour mills, because one could steal flour, hiding it in one's clothing. The theft was not always successful, since there was police at the gate, with whom, at best, one would have to share the loot. At other times the night's work was lost, as they took away everything. They did not confiscate it for the state, but for themselves. I am still grateful to a manager of one small flour mill, who, anxious to help a fellow Jew, kept on hiring me night after night, until he was reassigned.

The stolen flour was a treasure. I was able to use it to get living quarters, or at least lodgings for the night. Living space was extremely difficult to get in Chkalov at that time. The official evacuees were assigned quarters in local residents' flats. People like me had to fend for themselves. I was lodged for some time in a pit, one of many such, dug out in the clay works. I was a paying lodger of a Russian woman whose husband was away in a forced labor camp as a criminal. Her son belonged to a local gang of petty criminals. His "friendship" came in handy when I lost my ration cards in a poker game. They were returned to me; I would have starved otherwise. I was less lucky sometime later, when my ration cards were stolen by a pickpocket from a different gang. Chkalov was full of gangs. Especially dangerous were the juvenile gangs, armed with long razors, who would think nothing of slashing the face of anybody they suspected of witnessing their crimes. I had to leave these quarters because a criminal occupying the next pit suspected me of carrying on with the woman he lived with. (This was not true.)

At harvest time, on days off, I would try to supplement my income by bringing melons from Ilek and selling them in the bazaar. I would do it by hitching rides on trucks going toward Ilek and buying the melons from owners of small garden plots, whom I had known previously. One such attempt at hitching a ride ended in disaster for me. As I was boarding a truck from the rear, the driver jerked his truck ahead, throwing me to the ground. I must have lost consciousness, and when I came to I was lying all alone on the road, my thigh bleeding profusely. The thigh must have been ripped by some protruding piece of iron on the truck. I managed to get up, pressing the ripped flesh as hard as I could. I walked back in the direction of Chkalov — for how long, I don't remember. By a stroke of luck, I saw a sign of a military hospital. This was forbidden territory for a civilian, I knew, but I had no choice. I rang the bell at the guard house and begged them to let me in. To my great surprise they did, and the medics on duty treated my wound. Bandages were scarce, but they sprayed the hanging flesh with some unknown substance, which acted as an adhesive. I don't remember how I got back to the quarters that I was occupying at that time.

I had a nice landlady then, an older widow, in whose two- room flat I was renting a bed. I stayed in that bed for days, in considerable pain after the original shock wore off. She must have taken care of me at first, before I was able to communicate with a woman I had known in Ilek. That woman came with provisions and took over my care for a few days. As I was young my wound did not take long to heal. The medics in the hospital must have done a good job cleansing the open wound with just soap and water. Shock prevented me from feeling the pain of such an operation. Some pain at the site of the injury has remained with me, especially when there are changes in the weather. As soon as I could, I returned to work at my factory. How I managed to excuse my absence, I don't remember. Absences from work were a criminal offence.

During 1943 I was able to exchange communications with my father by letter and by telegram. He also sent me packages with clothing. I used some of the contents and traded the rest for food at the bazaar. I resumed my occasional trips to Ilek as soon as I recovered. On one such trip, during the winter, I was dropped off somewhere on the road, halfway between Chkalov and Ilek, and started the rest of the way on foot. I was caught in a sudden snowstorm, which was not unusual in that area. I kept on walking, in a complete whiteout, in the middle of the unpopulated steppe. I kept thinking of home, of my mother, and of the end of the war. At times I was certain that I would freeze right there on the road and that nobody would find my corpse under the snow until springtime. A miracle happened, however. In the whiteout, I almost bumped into a large truck. This was one of a score of American Lend-Lease trucks stuck there in the snowstorm. The drivers must have all left, abandoning the trucks, leaving the cab doors open. This was a lifesaver for me. I got into one of the cabs and, safe from the falling snow, I waited out the blizzard. I eventually reached Ilek.

There were many Polish refugees in Chkalov. I became friendly with one of them, a young man from Tarnów. Before the war, Klieger (whose first name I don't remember) was an apprentice tailor, but on holidays he used to sing in the synagogue. In Chkalov, he was able to get a job as a soloist with a municipal orchestra. His main job consisted of intoning songs of praise for Stalin. His position was important enough to get him and his Russian wife a one-room apartment that they had all to themselves, an unheard-of luxury in wartime Chkalov. His food ration was higher than mine. At least a couple of times I was a "dinner" guest at their apartment. Later, in 1944, when former Polish citizens started getting permission to return home, Klieger told me that he intended to stay. By this time, we suspected that we would probably have neither a home nor a family to return to. This was surely a factor in his decision.

By 1944, there were many wounded soldiers in Chkalov hospitals. These people seemed to be less afraid of the authorities than the general population and upon release from the hospitals they communicated the truth about the war. The Soviet Army offensive was then in full force. Large territories were liberated. From the soldiers who were with the liberating units one could find out many facts omitted from the official reports. The Jewish veterans were not sparing in their descriptions of the Holocaust. They described the empty shtetls in the Ukraine, whose inhabitants had been victims of mass murder beginning as early as June 1941. Somewhat later the first reports of the concentration camps began to come in. (Herman

Ladner, my father, told me, after we were reunited, about having participated in a mass demonstration of 20,000 Jews in Madison Square Garden in New York City, to put pressure on President Roosevelt to do something about rescuing Jews in German occupied territories. Not until 1944 was the War Refugee Board established.)

It was in the summer of 1944, I think, that I was the victim of an anti-Semitic attack. While I was walking on the main street of the city two passing young soldiers started hitting me with their fists while shouting anti-Semitic epithets. When I was down on the ground they kicked me for good measure. I wasn't really injured, but my feelings were hurt. Anybody who wore eyeglasses was suspected of being a Jew. (Luckily my glasses did not break. I could not have managed without them, and replacing them was out of the question.) Except for that one kick by a Nazi soldier in 1939, I had never been physically attacked as a Jew until that time.

This was nothing, of course, by comparison with the Nazi atrocities that by then I had become aware of. I was raring to go and get revenge. As soon as the Soviet-allied Polish Army was beginning to be formed, I tried to volunteer for it. (The previously formed Polish Army, under General Anders, would not accept Jewish volunteers. At least, this was the rumor spread by the Soviet authorities. There is still some controversy on this subject. The Anders Army was allowed to join the Western Allies by going through Iran to Palestine.) In a letter of September 5, 1944, to my father, I wrote that I planned to join the Berling Army[15] on the following day. It seems that I was not accepted; perhaps the Soviet medical commission rejected me again. I no longer remember the details. At any rate, I remained in Chkalov.

---

15 The Soviet-approved "Polish People's Army," commanded by Major General Zygmunt Berling.

Toward the end of the war, I was reassigned to a construction unit. At first, we worked within the plant, but later, we were transferred to various municipal sites; for example, we constructed a nursery school and worked on the renovation of the Chkalov Opera House. My work usually consisted of preparing concrete, sometimes by mixing cement manually and sometimes by operating a small mixer. This work was considered unhealthy, so I was allotted a ration of American-supplied soybean milk, which was supposed to counteract the accumulation of harmful dust in my lungs. Later on I was made an assistant to a plasterer who promised to teach me the craft. On these jobs we often worked alongside groups of German prisoners of war. As angry as I was at the Germans, I couldn't help feeling pity for those emaciated prisoners in their tattered uniforms. At least once I gave one bread and at another time a cigarette. While they were guarded, they were not completely isolated from other workers.

It was possible for me to be so "generous" because by then the supply situation had improved. The bread ration was increased, and it was possible to buy food at the bazaar (including American canned meat, Spam, a delicacy). Also, in 1945, those registered with the Polish Committee received an extra ration of bread. This was white bread, which was considered a luxury. At the end of July 1945, I received a package from my father, the last one to reach me in the Soviet Union.

In the summer of 1945, the repatriation of Polish citizens began. It didn't seem to matter that most of them had been forced to receive Soviet citizenship. This was the time when my Uncle Fredek showed up in Chkalov to register for repatriation. Now we were together again, but we didn't return to Poland at the same time. Aron Osterweil also appeared in Chkalov. True to his nature, he did not wait for any kind of official repatriation; even before the end of the war, he had somehow made his way to Romania after the Germans withdrew from there. (The next time I saw him was in 1969 in Eilat, on my first trip to Israel.)

It was not until the spring of 1946 that my turn came to be repatriated. It was another long trip by railroad, but this time it was in passenger cars. The cars were overcrowded with people and their possessions. My possessions consisted of one small bag, with my school certificates from Tarnów and Lwów, some photographs, and perhaps a few pieces of clothing. We were given some food for the trip, which was not sufficient for the long journey. The long train seemed to have been unguarded, but there must have some armed escorts travelling with us. They proved useful when, just after crossing the new Polish border, we heard an exchange of gunfire. Our train, like many other such trains bringing mostly Jewish returnees, was attacked by one of the underground Polish anti-Semitic bands. (More about them later.) The destination of the train was Lower Silesia, "recovered territories," where the repatriates were being settled in place of the expelled German population. I, however, decided to jump the train in Tarnów. With a mixture of joy and sorrow, I spotted the turret of the building where my family had lived, before we got to the Tarnów station. I missed, however, another prominent sight, that of the cupola of the New Synagogue.[16]

By this time, I had practically no hope of finding my mother or my brothers alive. I said practically, because some hope remained with me for weeks thereafter. Like many other Jews, I posted notes on the bulletin board of the Tarnów Jewish Committee, hoping that at least my brother Henek would appear.

---

16   The New Synagogue of Tarnów opened in August of 1908. It was burned and blown up by the Nazis in November of 1939.

Soon I found out that all the newcomers in Tarnów were, like myself, people repatriated from the Soviet Union. The camps had been liberated months before and those in hiding or on alien papers had also reappeared.

I knew the Tarnów Jewish Committee was located on Goldhammer Street, as I had corresponded with them from Chkalov. On my there, I stopped at 13 Krakowska Street. The building looked the same as I had remembered it. The corner store was occupied by the widow of its prewar owner, a Pole, who had been killed by the Germans. Mrs. Lewandowska seemed glad to see me. My visit was not unexpected, as my father had already written to her about my return. The store, which had specialized in fancy foods before the war, was beginning to get restocked with foods, albeit more common ones. I did get some food from Mrs. Lewandowska but not much other support. She had agreed to become my father's agent in administering the building, but she had no right to give me living quarters in the building.

I wanted very much to live again in my father's house, but it took a good deal of time and effort on my part to accomplish this. With the help of Dr. Lubieniecki, a well-known Polish lawyer, whose client my father had once been, I managed to get an audience with the mayor of the city. Dr. Lubieniecki, who among his clients had also had Sanguszko, the local prince, had returned from a Nazi camp quite recently and was just reestablishing his law practice. The audience with the mayor proved to be a success. Jerky Sito, one of the leaders of the Socialist Party in Tarnów, turned out to have known my father. (Years later I found out that Sito had been imprisoned for political reasons.) Thanks to his intervention, I got a one-room apartment on the fourth floor of my father's house. I don't remember having a bathroom there, but there was a gas range. For washing, I walked up one floor to the laundry room of the building. The janitor, Polar (Apolune) Kocik, was the widow of the prewar janitor, who was killed by the Germans — for helping Jews, she said. She arranged for me to tutor her adopted daughter in elementary arithmetic. The lessons took place in my one-room apartment, with Mrs. Kocik always present. I don't know whether she wanted to protect her daughter from a Jew or from a returnee from the Godless Soviet Union. I spotted some of our oil paintings hanging on the wall of the Kocik basement apartment, but I did not remark on it to her.

It took some time, however, before I could move in. In the meantime, I had to share dormitory-style quarters on Lwowska Street with other Jewish returnees. The quarters were provided by the Jewish Committee, located not far away, which also provided us with meals. The whole network of Jewish Committees in Poland was funded by the "Joint" (Jewish Joint Distribution Committee). The head of the Jewish Committee in Tarnów at that time, who also had returned from USSR, was Mr. Kornilo, a dental technician. He had been a long-time member of the Bund, which advocated for the development of Jewish secular culture in Eastern Europe, in opposition to the Zionist movement, which had been for mass emigration to Palestine. By that time, Mr. Kornilo had renounced his Bundist ideology, which had prevented very many Jews from leaving Poland when it was possible to do so.

Palestine was my preferred destination, too — either that or staying put in Poland, which, however, was out of the question. Somewhat reluctantly I had to accede to my father's repeated requests, by letter and by telegram, to join him in America. He was working hard at getting at least a student visa for me. In the meantime, he transferred small amounts of money to me through Polish-American officials travelling to Poland. He said that if I wouldn't agree to join him in America he would return to Poland. Among the people warning against returning were friends from Tarnów, Mr. and Mrs. Spiller, with whom he was in correspondence. They had married after the war, their previous spouses having fallen victim to the Nazis. I was a guest of the Spillers a number of times, in their nice apartment on Krakowska Street. This was a pleasant change from the Jewish Committee dormitory environment.

This was a transitional period in Poland, before the Communist Party became the sole ruler, and small businesses were still allowed to operate. Mr. Spiller, for example, was able to recover possession of his suitcase factory in Tarnów. Another beneficiary of this liberal policy was a former schoolmate of mine, Pelek Fessel, who survived the war on Aryan papers, then returned to Tarnów and opened a successful roofing-paper factory. Pelek had taken part in the Polish Warsaw uprising in 1944 as an officer of the Home Army. Only his commanding officers knew that he was Jewish. I lost touch with Pelek but had a brief reunion with him in 1964 when our classmate Haskel Kurz sought us both out in New York. By a strange coincidence, Pelek's only daughter and I were graduate students at Yale at the same time. Unfortunately, he developed cancer and died shortly after our reunion.

One of my former schoolmates in Tarnów at that time was Lusia Weg. Not only had she been in my class at Safah Berurah but we had also been in the same unit of the Zionist youth organization, Gordonia.[17] Her family had been well-to-do and owned a distillery

---

17 Gordonia was a Zionist youth movement that followed the teachings of A. D. Gordon, who advocated the redemption of the Land of Israel and the Jewish people through manual labor and the revival of Hebrew.

in Tarnów. Lusia had been in the Tarnów ghetto, managed to escape, and survived with the help of a Polish friend of her family. After the war, she married another student from Safah Berurah, who had survived on Aryan papers. Somehow, somewhere, he learned the profession of dentistry and had a practice in Tarnów. After I left Tarnów, they moved to Western Poland, where his practice flourished. In 1956 they decided to emigrate to Israel. Their belongings had already been loaded on a ship leaving for Israel when Lusia's husband suddenly died of a heart attack. Devastated, Lusia and her small son returned to Wrocław. I lost contact with her until 1991, when she met us in Tarnów along with our old friend Dalek (Spielman) Adler, who came from Sweden to meet us. In 1994 or 1995, Lusia with her son and his family liquidated their possessions in Wrocław and finally made aliyah to Israel.

My old schoolmates were not the only people I socialized with in Tarnów. It was difficult for me to become friendly with former inmates of the camps, since I found them different, extremely materialistic, even rapacious, but I found friends among repatriates with experiences similar to mine. (To this day I feel bad sometimes about not having been more sympathetic to the camp survivors' plight, but those I happened to meet were all engaged in shady deals, in the black market, and even in such rackets as taking over real estate that had belonged to deceased Jews unrelated to them.) There was a girl in the dormitory, a member of a family of returnees from Kazakhstan, who became my steady companion during my stay in Tarnów. We would take long walks together to all the places I remembered going to before the war, to the town park, to the surrounding meadows, to the hill called St. Martin's Mountain. We had fun, and I must have suppressed my sadness somehow. Unlike almost all other Jews, who spoke constantly of Tarnów and Poland as "one big cemetery," I was enjoying myself. I was happy to have enough food to eat (even chocolate, thanks to my father), to have leisure, to speak my native tongue, read newspapers, and so on — all the things I had lacked for six or seven long years. (For a whole week after arrival in Tarnów I ate enormous quantities of cherries, which were arriving at the market then.) I was only 23 years old. I wanted to have a good time. Of course, I felt guilty of "dancing on the cemetery." I still do. But youth has its rights.

I did attend all the commemorative ceremonies that took place at the several sites of mass murder in Tarnów and vicinity. The biggest such event took place at the Jewish cemetery, where a monument was erected to the Jewish victims of the Nazis. The sculptor of the monument was a fellow resident of the dormitory who later went to Israel and became well known.[18] (The gate of the Tarnów cemetery was donated by the Polish President, Lech Walesa, to the Holocaust Museum in Washington. A copy was manufactured in Tarnów and erected in place of the original one.)

A couple of times I traveled to the big city, Krakow, to view the sights. Once I even visited a cabaret, for the first time in my life. Such train trips had their dangers. This was a time of near civil war in Poland. There was armed resistance to the Communists who were, with Soviet assistance, taking power from a quasi-coalition government. As Jews were considered the allies of the Communists (as they had been before the war, too), they often fell victims to the various insurgent bands. There were pogroms in some cities. (It is said that some 1,000 Jews were killed before 1948.) Bands would stop trains and kill Jewish passengers. Sometimes on my trips I tried to get friendly with young female Polish passengers to escape being

---

18 Sculptor David Becker used a piece taken from the ruins of the Jubilee Synagogue to create the monument.

identified. However, I never actually found myself in any danger.

Twice, at least, I had to go to Warsaw, to appear before the American consul in connection with my father's efforts to obtain a student visa for me. It was quite shocking to see Warsaw in ruins. The reconstruction had not begun yet. It was in Warsaw that I got my first post-war haircut. The barber was using a straight razor. Considering the level of anti-Semitism in Poland at that time, I was afraid that he might cut my throat.

My host on my first trip to Warsaw was a second cousin, Ferdynand Chaber (previously Haber). I must have gotten his address while I was yet in Tarnów, though I don't remember where or how, because I walked there straight from the barber shop. The building he lived in was a large structure in the center of the city, either untouched by the war or already restored. I was very surprised to find armed guards at the entrance, who had to announce me to my cousin before they allowed me to enter the building. The building housed important Communist Party offices, and the Chabers occupied a large apartment on one of the upper floors. I remembered Chaber's wife from my pre-war visit to the American consulate: Dora Gutter was my cousin's Party comrade. My cousin, a lawyer, was then in jail as a political prisoner (the Communist Party being illegal in pre-war Poland), so Dora had hosted me. She took me to the Jewish section of Warsaw, which was an exotic sight for me, the noisy teeming streets, thousands of little stores with Yiddish signs, and the sound of Yiddish being spoken all around me. She also took me to see The Great Dictator, a Charlie Chaplin movie satirizing Hitler, which, in August, 1939, was the rage of the town.

By 1946, the family had returned from the Soviet Union with a little baby, Helena (now the second-in-command of the largest newspaper in Poland). They had quarters in that building because my cousin was a high official in the Communist Party in Poland. He headed the political censorship office. He was glad to see me and very hospitable, to the point of handing me top-secret news bulletins to read. The Chabers tried to convince me not to go to America, to stay in Poland, which they said would be different, better than the pre-war Poland. They even offered me financial support to attend the University of Warsaw. My admission, they told me, was assured. With gratitude, of course, I declined the offer, as my father was eagerly awaiting me in New York.

Forty-five years later, in 1991, we again visited the Chabers, who were by then living in a desirable apartment building near the villas of the foreign ambassadors. Ferdynand Chaber, retired, owned his own spacious apartment, his neighbors being other retired high Party officials. He had been removed from the governing body of the Communist Party (known as the Polish Workers' Party) some years before when he refused to denounce his children for their membership in the Solidarity movement. (His son is a professor of mathematics at the University of Warsaw.) Although Ferdynand did not agree with his children's political platform, he was proud of not having denounced them. He remained a staunch Communist, albeit a "liberal" one. He, like many who identified themselves as Jews again after 1989, considered himself a "cultural" Jew. He tended to speak in clichés, as if he were delivering a propaganda speech. Despite his love of the "workers," he was not impressed by my stressing my career as a linotype operator, like the first Polish Communist president, Bolesław Bierut. At the urging of my family, I disclosed to him that I had been granted a PhD from Yale University. He threw his arms around me and cried, "The Jewish genes have triumphed!" I corresponded with him after returning to the U.S.in 1991, and he would send me long political tracts. Though I have not heard from him directly for the last couple of years, I inquired about him from Adam Michnik (editor-in-chief of the Polish newspaper *Gazeta Wyborcza*, Helena Chaber Luczywo's boss and close friend) when he came to speak at Yale University. Michnik assured me that Chaber was still alive and active.

The second time I visited Warsaw was in January 1947 to obtain my Swedish transit visa. I stayed overnight in a small one-room apartment, with a former schoolmate, Greisman, who was then a member of the secret police. He proudly showed me the Russian revolver he carried and the rifle in his closet. He was active in the units that fought the Ukrainian and Polish insurgents. Since most of them were militantly anti-Jewish, he was happy in his work. He told me that he was going to leave soon for Palestine, but a few years ago I heard that he remained in Poland and died of some illness.

I also journeyed by train to Lower Silesia in the new Recovered Territories. My father had sent me the address of his cousin's widow, Rivka Ladner. The cousin had been killed by the Nazis, but Rivka with their three young daughters managed to survive. Helped no doubt by their "non-Jewish looks" (and by not being circumcised males), they were able to "pass" as non-Jewish. Sometimes they were hidden. Having all grown up in a village, their Polish speech was free of Yiddishisms and they were familiar with farm work. All four of them had often been employed by farmers, though never together, to conceal the fact that they were members of the same family. They were reunited at the end of the war and moved to the New Territories, where the government was resettling Jews. They somehow obtained a villa in a Wałbrzych, formerly Waldenberg. The German inhabitants of the town, and of the villa, had been expelled when the Poles took over. The Ladner family "inherited" not only the villa with its garden but all its contents.

I was very well received and I stayed with them a number of days. Although I had never heard of them before the war, which was the case with most of my father's family, it was a pleasant visit. I was well fed, slept in a real bed, and generally enjoyed the bourgeois setting, which reminded me of home. I also enjoyed the company of the three attractive girls, the oldest of whom, Jadzia, was my favorite. She, however, had a boyfriend, a Jewish officer in the Polish Army. (She must have broken off with him later, as she married someone else, with whom she emigrated to France.) Rivka Ladner was nudging me towards friendship with her middle daughter, Bronka. When I wrote to my father about it, he got very upset. Until I left Poland, he insisted in all his letters that I remain single until I join him. A couple of years later, Rivka and her two daughters were brought to America by Rivka's relatives. They lived in Brooklyn and contacted me from there. Wary of further involvement, I did not maintain the contact even though I was grateful for their hospitality in Poland.

While I was in Lower Silesia I travelled to its main city, Wrocław, formerly Breslau, to enroll in the medical school then being established there. Previously, in Tarnów, I had passed a number of examinations given to students who, because of the war, had not managed to obtain their Matura certificate, which would have entitled them to enter university. That document entitled me to enter a medical school. I was accepted to the medical school in Wrocław, but instead of enrolling I left the country. Wrocław had been fought over by the opposing armies and was one vast ruin. With my angry feelings toward Germans, I was not unhappy with the ruination, which seemed worse than Warsaw. (Warsaw had been wantonly destroyed by the Germans after the failed Polish uprising of 1944.[19])

On July 9, 1946, I registered for the draft but was freed from military duty because of my myopia. I was then free to emigrate if and when my American visa came through. Large numbers of Jews were leaving Poland, usually by being smuggled across the Czechoslovakian border, for the Displaced Persons camps in Germany. Formally their passage was illegal, though all the governments involved, including the Poles, were closing their eyes to it. (A year or so later the Poles closed the border to keep their Jewish citizens within the country, as they were considered sympathetic to the new all-Communist government.) I, however, had a strong feeling against illegal border crossing. I don't know why I felt that way, but I decided to wait until I could emigrate legally. The wait stretched on longer and longer. Finally some papers from America arrived. On that basis, on September 18, 1946, I received a Polish passport valid for "United States of North America." As it turned out, I still could not go directly to the United States; I had to get a Swedish transit visa and go to Sweden first.

I received a visa on January 10, 1947, from the Swedish consul in Warsaw and left from the Warsaw airport for Sweden on January 25, 1947. This was my first air flight, and I was quite thrilled by it. I had a suitcase with me, but no money except for a five-dollar bill hidden in my clothes. There was a prohibition against taking foreign currency out of Poland, and the zloty was not convertible. I had an address in Stockholm; I don't remember how I obtained it. It was the address of a young Tarnów girl, Rutka Weiss, the daughter of a well-known physician, who had gone to Sweden with a transport of

---

19 The Warsaw Uprising by the Polish underground in the summer of 1944 followed the Warsaw Ghetto Uprising of April–May, 1943. By January, 1945, the Germans had destroyed most of Warsaw.

young Jewish women rescued from Nazi labor camps just before the end of the war. I considered the address a treasured possession, as I was wary of arriving in a strange city, in a foreign country, whose language I did not know. The other worry was my lack of money. It would be some time, I knew, until my father could send me some.

My lack of money proved troublesome as soon as I got off the plane. I had nothing with which to pay for my transportation from the airport to the city. I didn't realize how far it was and anyway I had no choice. I walked and walked, dragging my suitcase, and finally reached Stockholm. My troubles were not over yet. Holding Rutka's address scribbled on a piece of paper, I kept reading it to everybody I met. I read it in different ways, switching the accent in the five-syllable name of the street from one syllable to another. For a long time this method was of no help. Nobody could understand what I was saying, and the written address was no help either. Finally, one of the several policemen I badgered, who had more linguistic imagination than the others, was able to direct me to Skepparegatan. I was dead tired by the time I finally arrived at the pension where Rutka was staying.

It turned out that she was not the only Polish Jew who was given lodgings there. I recognized at least two Tarnów names: One was that of Elek Volkman, whose father, now deceased, had a bad reputation in the Jewish Committee, having served on the *Judenrat*. The others were a mother and son, the Polaneckis. Both Polaneckis had gone through Nazi camps and were the only survivors of their family. Rutka, too, was the only survivor of her family, having lost her mother, father, and younger brother. Among other camps, she had worked in Plaszów, near Krakow, known to all from the movie *Schindler's List*. Elek Volkman, Joseph Polanecki, and Rutka Weiss were all about the same age, the age of my brother Henek.

Rutka had been a pupil in the nursery school in Tarnów run by my Aunt Hela before the war. Rutka's mother had been active in Zionist circles and returned to Tarnów from an international congress in Switzerland just before the outbreak of the war. Had she not returned she would have been saved. Elek, Rutka, and Joseph with his mother eventually settled in New York. I was friendly with Joseph for a while, but lost contact with him after he married. He became the owner of a garment factory and prospered. He died of a heart attack several years ago. I had no contact with Elek until 1995 when we exchanged telephone calls and discussed the possibility of going to a reunion of the Tarnów Jews that was to take place in Israel. He had become a prosperous dealer in diamonds. Rutka (Weiss) Merdinger was divorced and has two children; they all live in the New York City area. She visited us in Connecticut, and we speak occasionally by phone.)

Rutka was very glad to see me. She had somehow been prepared for my arrival and had arranged for me to have a room in the pension. She was very valuable to me. She introduced me to all the Swedes, with whom we shared the dining room, and to the customs at the table, which were different from everything I had seen before. By the time I arrived, Rutka had become familiar with the Swedish language and served as my interpreter. I had thought that the language, being Germanic, would be easy. On my walk through the city, on the day of my arrival, I was able to understand many of the printed signs. What I had not realized was the difficulty of pronouncing the consonant clusters and, especially, the intonation, which proved most difficult for me to master.

Stockholm was a wonder city to me. It was untouched by war, Sweden having been neutral. Most of the city, the modern part, had broad streets, well lit, and lined with fantastic illuminated store fronts. Never before had I seen anything like it. Behind the store-fronts were stores filled with all kinds of merchandise. I had my first post-war oranges in Stockholm. Coffee houses and sweets shops were full of customers. Once I even went to a wondrous multilevel coffee house, where men and women had a unique way of communicating with each other across the halls and on different levels. Every table had a prominently displayed number and a telephone used for that purpose. I was there with a young woman from Finland who was introducing me to the city. We spoke to each other in broken German.

The old part of the city was equally fascinating to me. The streets were narrow and curvy, and many of the buildings dated to the Middle Ages. The harbor was nearby, with ships coming and going and the king's castle just across the water. All of this was lit at night. I had plenty of time to explore Stockholm, since usually people on transit visas were not allowed to work in Sweden. Not until March of 1947 was I able to get a work permit. My financial situation improved then. The money I had been getting from my father was barely sufficient to pay for my room and board in the pension. When my Uncle Fredek joined me at the pension, after having been in a DP camp in Germany, he paid half the rent for our room.

I found a job in a large machine-building factory on the outskirts of Stockholm. The main output of the plant was farm machinery. The company, Separator Werke, was named for its chief product, milk separators. I was hired as an unskilled worker and assigned to the transport of parts from one division to another. Although my work classification remained "transport worker," after a while I was assisting at testing the finished product. I used my high-school German to read the manuals printed in that language. By that time I knew just enough Swedish to communicate with my fellow workers.

I never became proficient in the language, but I could understand headlines in the newspapers.

During my stay in Stockholm, at my father's insistence (and with his money) I studied English. I had found a former teacher of English from Warsaw, who drilled me in the British pronunciation. I also studied something else: ballroom dancing. I made little progress and quit after a few lessons. The ballroom dancing was not my father's idea. Before leaving the country, I went, with Josek Polanecki, to a department store, where I bought a suit, a shirt, a tie and pajamas. (I still have the pajamas.) The navy blue, pinstriped suit was double-breasted and, in my eyes, very elegant. My Uncle Fredek taught me how to knot a tie, but I hadn't really learned the technique until my cousin Don taught it to me in the Bronx. I was very proud of that suit until some years later, when my wife and her sister made fun of me in my Swedish suit.

On April 16, 1947, Carl Birkeland, the American vice-consul in Stockholm, issued a non-quota visa for me, and I was ready to go join my father in New York. The train ride from Stockholm to the port of Gothenburg was very picturesque. Unlike my previous train trips, this one was enjoyable. The railroad cars were elegant, with large windows from which I could admire the Swedish countryside. The ship I boarded, the Gripsholm, was the namesake of another one that had been lost during the war. My father booked passage for me in the cabin class, which was above tourist class. My cabinmate was a demobilized British flier who did not want to stay in England and was travelling all over the world trying to find a place for himself. I practiced my English on him, and we got very friendly. He introduced me to the ship's bar and its cocktails. I had never had mixed drinks before, and I liked this novelty. I didn't suffer from seasickness as I was half-drunk for most of the voyage. All of this, of course, on my father's money. I had not realized how limited my father's means were. I did find time during the five-day voyage to get acquainted with another fellow passenger, an attractive Dutch girl. We had a good time together until I made some unfavorable remark about the Dutch royalty; she wouldn't speak to me after that, until we arrived in New York.

When we arrived in the port of New York on April 30, 1947, my Dutch friend and almost all the passengers disembarked. I was among the few left on the deck. From the height of the deck, I could see my father on the pier, together with my cousin Lillian. My father recognized me, and I recognized him. He expected me to join him on the pier and when I shouted to him that for some reason I was not allowed to get off the boat and that I might be sent back, he started crying and so did Lillian. They stayed on the pier for some time, until the pier was completely empty. It took a long time before I was informed that, instead of getting off in New York, I would be taken to Ellis Island for investigation. Then and for years afterwards, I assumed that I was being held back as a politically suspect arrival. However, the reason probably was the Immigration Service's suspicion that my student visa was a ploy only and I really intended to permanently stay in the United States where my father was residing.

My situation on Ellis Island was hardly upsetting to me. I had seen dormitories before, and this one was luxurious by comparison. The food was satisfactory, although not as good as the food given to those who declared themselves Orthodox Jews. Their Kosher food was supplied by New York Jewish organizations. The place was not teeming with immigrants, as it had been in previous years, when immigration was at its peak. By the time I arrived, there were some empty halls. We were all examined by a team of doctors, who were looking for defects or illnesses that would prohibit our admittance to the United States. I passed the physical examination, then began a series of interviews with the immigration officials. After the first day, I would be taken by motorboat to the harbor, and from there, escorted by an immigration officer, by subway to the Upper West Side of New York City. There, at the headquarters of the Immigration Service, I underwent daily grueling interviews. I had the same escorting officer all the time, who asked me if I was Jewish and tried to have a Yiddish conversation with me. He was friendly enough to treat me to candy from vending machines in the subway.

It was not good to be introduced to New York City through its subway system. I was shocked at the mobs of pushing passengers, the noise, and the dirt in the subway. Another shocking sight was the view from the elevated parts of the system. The buildings I could see from the Third Avenue El seemed old and decrepit, nothing like the pictures of the city in the New York World's Fair brochures that my father had sent us to Tarnów in 1939. Unlike my father, I was somehow not terribly upset by the delay. It was a new experience, I was not treated harshly (unlike elsewhere in the past), and I was sure that I would eventually be admitted.

Throughout this time, my father and cousin Lillian were making great efforts to help my case. Lillian provided a new affidavit, showing her bank account and stating that she would support me financially. They also contacted any politician that they thought might assist them in their efforts. All this activity, including my apparently correct answers, helped. On May 9, 1947, after a bond was filed, I was admitted as a Student under Section 4 (e), Immigration Act of 1924. The expiration date of this visa was May 9, 1948.

Finally, after eight years and four months, I was reunited with my father. Of course we felt a great deal of both happiness and sadness. There was also some disappointment on both sides. My father was disappointed that I was not an observant Jew: I smoked on the Sabbath, I didn't pray daily, and so on. I was disappointed by my father's financial situation and living conditions. My father was a boarder in the apartment of his sister Rae, whose daughter Lillian, on her secretary's salary, was her mother's sole support. I remembered my father as the real head of our household, with all the powers that went with it. He set the tone, he made the rules, he was obeyed. Here he had to be grateful to his sister for allowing him to live there, and he had to abide by her rules. (It must be said, however, that to please my father Rae kept a strictly Kosher household.) It wasn't long before I had some clashes with my aunt. Neither her apartment nor her household was anything like what I remembered from before the war. Though it surely was incomparably better than the situations I found myself in during the war, the apartment was smaller than the ones we and our relatives had had in Tarnów. It was crammed with heavy furniture, in a style I disliked, which was usually protected by plastic covers. Once, at least, I was severely reprimanded for putting my feet on the couch. Now, I think that I must have reacted to my changed circumstances. While I was with my father, I did not feel at home, which I probably resented. From the beginning, therefore, I may have acted more independently than I should have.

Cousin Lillian was very friendly. She used to take me around town, which meant taking the subway to Manhattan, since their apartment was in the Bronx. I saw my first post-war American movies with Lillian, and she treated me to ice-cream in a local candy store. We had long conversations, which helped me with my English.

Both Lillian and my father helped me make the rounds of our relatives. Almost all of them lived in the New York City area, in the Bronx and in Brooklyn. The aunts, uncles, and cousins were full of pity for the "refugee" and were astounded that I could speak to them in their own language. Sometimes they couldn't understand some of my too-literary vocabulary. They were generous with their hospitality, feeding me sumptuous meals (like roast goose), as they thought that I was too skinny. They also gave me pocket money, for which I was thankful, as I had none.

As a holder of a student visa, I was prohibited from gainful employment except during summer vacations. While at first my father had enrolled me in a yeshiva, due to my vehement objection, I ended up being admitted to a prep school. I entered Eron Preparatory School, located at Broadway and 14th Street in New York City, as soon as the semester began. I had to pass an entrance examination to enable the school to place me. As I had already finished my secondary education, I benefitted only from the courses in the English language and in American literature. My father managed to convince his sister Fanny's husband, Sam Velger, to arrange a summer job in the Catskills, where Sam was employed as a waiter. I spent my second summer in the United States working as a busboy in the Swan Lake Hotel in Ferndale. The work was hard, the hours were long, but I was glad to be able to save some money. I also developed friendships with the other staff, which consisted mainly of New York City college students. It surprised me that college students had to work.

After a couple of summers of such work, I had enough money saved to move out of the Bronx apartment and find my own quarters. I enjoyed being independent and on my own again. I was also glad that my father did not have to spend his hard-earned money on the upkeep of his grown son. My father worked hard indeed. He was employed as a shipping clerk in a Manhattan stationery store. The owners kept reminding him that they were doing him a favor by employing him, as he refused to work on Saturdays and Jewish holidays. Once, when he was ill, I substituted for him; after a few days, my father was told that my work was not satisfactory and that he would lose his job if he did not return. My Soviet work experience did not prepare me for employment in a private firm with its demands. I was shocked to see how hard my father had to work.

My father died on December 22, 1968. Though he was very proud of his grandchildren and got great pleasure from them, he was not happy that my wife and I were not observant Jews and did not approve of our membership in a Reform congregation. For example, he adored his granddaughter Susan but did not recognize the validity of her bat mitzvah ceremony and would not attend the celebration. (He did give her a very beautiful gold bracelet, but he emphasized that it was for her birthday.) He also did not attend his grandson Mark's bar mitzvah, because it was in the same Reform temple. He did arrange for Mark to celebrate becoming a bar mitzvah a second time, this time at an Orthodox shul, for which my father prepared him, taught him to put on phylacteries (*tefillin*), and bought Mark his own set. Unfortunately, my father died before his youngest grandchild, Frederick, was old enough to become bar mitzvah.

Although my father did not live long enough to see me receive my PhD, he had the satisfaction of knowing that I was enrolled in a doctoral program at Yale University and was happy knowing that, so many years after his leaving Tarnów, some of his aspirations for me were being fulfilled.

Acknowledgments

Many family members and friends were generous with their time and helped to validate these stories and shape the manuscript. Ewa provided me with firsthand memories of events, helped me understand the emotional aspects of the experiences they went through, and provided some color to my mother's descriptions, especially of our father. Being an avid reader, she gave me valuable advice on how to best tell our story.

Like Ewa, my cousin Josef gradually opened up about his own story, helped check my facts, and put the events he witnessed in the right perspective. We also worked together on the photographs for this book. In the course of searching for information on the internet, we discovered some photographs that have enriched our knowledge of our family history, such as a photograph of Israel Jakub Osterweil's tailoring shop from 1903. This was the first time Jerzyk or I had seen our grandfather's image.

I am grateful, too, to my cousin Avram Osterweil, who generously shared with me his notes and photographs, adding his memories to my thread of stories.

Shlomo Arad, the photographer I met in 2009 when he came to pay his respects at my mother's shiva, explained the role of the Hungarian fascists, the Arrow Cross party, in persecution of the Jews.

He told me how my father had found him and his brother under an overpass, brought them to shelter, and made sure they recovered and thrived. I am grateful for the kindness Shlomo showed by visiting my father years later, to thank him for all my father had done.

George Axelrod, may he rest in peace, added to my admiration of my dad by sharing the story of his survival under a pile of corpses in the Budapest ghetto to be picked up by my father's team and nursed to health in one of safe houses.

Miriam (Marisia) Offen opened my eyes to the real reason my father was saved at the *selektion* from being deported from the Janowska concentration camp to Belzec or Auschwitz.

Ed Herman, whom I found serendipitously during my search for information about the orphanage in Vác, shared his story and photographs.

Kuba Fleischer, an old friend from Hashomer Hatzair, eulogized my father at his funeral as a distinguished educator, a mentor, and Fleischer's inspiration as a Zionist and pioneer. Kuba had been one of the members of Hashomer Hatazair in Tarnów who had heeded Monek's advice and went to Brno, Czechoslovakia, to study agronomy, only to be expelled from the movement for defying the order to make *aliyah* first. (Eventually he returned to the movement and emigrated to Palestine in 1932.)

Special appreciation to my editors: Erika M. Steiger, who improved the manuscript considerably, and Joel Segel, whose excellent guiding questions and impressive depth of thinking were rooted in his understanding of the messages such stories convey to current and future generations that did not experience the Holocaust. Finally, I am grateful to my immediate family: To my wife, Dr. Erna Osterweil, for her support and understanding, and for tolerating my telling the story hundreds of times, and to our kids, Gali, Michal, and Amir, for their comments and constructive criticism.

Made in the USA
Las Vegas, NV
06 June 2022

49899565R00129